LIVING
WITH THE
RIBBON

LIVING

WITH THE

RIBBON

**A Teenagers Story About Battling
Cancer Through High School**

MacKenzie Greenberg

authorHOUSE®

AuthorHouse™
1663 Liberty Drive
Bloomington, IN 47403
www.authorhouse.com
Phone: 1 (800) 839-8640

Published by AuthorHouse 6/17/2015

ISBN: 978-1-5049-1619-6 (sc)
ISBN: 978-1-5049-1618-9 (e)

Library of Congress Control Number: 2015909080

Print information available on the last page.

To anyone and everyone who is living with the ribbon,
To my doctors and unconditional support systems, and
Above all, to my family
*You are all amazing; no words I put down in print will be able
to describe how much you have all influenced my life*

I cannot find the words to describe how much these people have assisted in this project or helped me along the way. You will never know how thankful I am for everything you have done...

Mrs. Amanda Eppley- Words cannot express my gratitude for all that you have done for me. Starting from joking about me writing a book, overseeing the project from start to finish, following the project from thousands of miles away, to always caring about me outside of the classroom. Thank you for your unwavering respect for my privacy and allowing me to trust you with this process. This would not have been possible without your understanding, your assistance, and your guidance. Thank you from the bottom of my heart.

Ms. Jill St. Martin- Despite being one of the biggest "pains", without a doubt, I would not have survived my four years at Hopedale High School without you. Through the "bad advice" and "professional bullying", you taught me that there's more to life than just what I wanted to think. Your attempts at opening me up and pulling me out of a state of denial eventually paid off. From your awkward questions to your patience and determination in trying to break me down and get me to put pride aside and let it happen, I am forever thankful. It may have taken you a couple of years and countless attempts, but you finally got me to utilize you for more than just the academics. If you hadn't haunted me all this time, I would not be who I am today. Thanks for always being an ear, helping with the academics, putting up with my shit for four years, and most importantly, for teaching me that it's ok to be vulnerable and put pride aside in the face of adversity. Almost everything you have said to me will forever be looked back on and remembered. The lessons you have taught me are more valuable than anything I could have ever imagined. Look how far we have come since the day you joked about me writing a book...

Ms. Jessica Ladieu- For a relationship that formed later in my high school years, you made an immediate impact on me. You instilled a sense of trust from the beginning that allowed me to continue athletics throughout the journey. Thank you for always encouraging me to stick with the things I love, convincing me that things will get better, supporting me unconditionally, building me up after I've been torn down, and always protecting the best interest of the student athletes. Your wise and encouraging words were always what I needed to get me through the tough times. I can't thank you enough for all that you have done for me in all aspects of life. I get to forever enjoy special memories because you forced me to make the decision that was right for me and not what everyone else wanted me to do.

The Tag Team- You both know who you are. As a pair, you deserve a special shout out. Without a doubt, you guys are the craziest people I have met. If your individual roles weren't enough, the combination of the two of you was added to the mix. Thank you for giving me that final push that I needed and above all, for being the most understanding and professional individuals I had the pleasure of meeting.

Ms. Caitlin McInnis- From your simple daily "Hello" in the hallway to your relentless positivity throughout the Field Hockey season and beyond, thank you. Positive people like you are the reason students and athletes grow. You create a learning environment both academically and athletically where people can thrive. From the very first time I met you as a substitute in sixth grade in Mendon- Upton, to freshman year when you and I both embarked on our journey at Hopedale High School, your positive attitude was always a source of aide in the time of need. As much as I couldn't stand it at the time, your constant check ins on the field to make sure I was ok were greatly appreciated. At the same time, thank you for never looking at me as an athlete faced with challenges and always allowing me to push myself to the limits.

Mrs. Lindsay Mayotte- Thank you for always being someone I could vent to, someone who I could trust completely, and someone who always respected my privacy. Most importantly, thank you for stepping in and overseeing this project senior year. This would not have been possible without your help.

Mrs. Kate Connors- Thank you for taking time out of your busy life to help with this process. Thank you for your willingness to assist in the gruesome task of editing a project you didn't even know existed until just months before the release of the final product.

Darlene Vittori Marsell- Although you had to be the bearer of bad news, you very easily are the one responsible for saving me. With no symptoms present despite the extensiveness of the cancer, who knows how bad things could have gotten before it was found. Following your gut even with my obvious dislike, makes me eternally grateful. From making yourself available whenever I may need you, to treating me like more than a patient, without you, I would not be who I am today.

Dr. Robert Shamberger-As a surgeon, you went out of your way to make my stubborn self understanding. You worked with me to make me as comfortable as possible and to ensure that I would continue to lead a normal life. Thank you for listening to me and hearing me out when most people would look at me like I was crazy, and most importantly, for always making an effort to put a smile on my face just minutes before going under and getting cut open.

Dr. Jessica Smith- I know I'm hands down one of your most difficult patients, but that has never turned you away from doing your best to figure out the best possible plan of action. Your relentless research and avid determination to come up with a treatment plan is admirable. I can't find the words to thank you for all that you have and all that you will continue to do. It took two years, but you really opened my eyes to what was actually going on, which allowed me to recognize the extent of how much had really occurred since the beginning of my journey with cancer.

All of my other support systems (nurses, doctors, friends, and teachers)- You all know who you are. Thank you for the texts, the visits, and everything else you did for me from diagnosis to the present. You are the ones who stuck with me through the toughest part of my life and I could not ever explain how much that means to me.

And last but not least, my family- I'm easily the worst patient to walk this earth. My family put up with me day in and day out despite this. Mom, I cannot imagine the pain this has caused you. No mother wants to watch their child suffer. You tried effortlessly to help me, even when I wouldn't help myself. You have always went out of your way to ensure that

I have everything I need and more. You will never understand how much I appreciate EVERYTHING you have done for me and all of the lessons you have taught me. Dad, Thank you allowing yourself to be my punching bag. You may be my father, but around you, I don't have to hide anything. Thank you for always believing in me and encouraging me to do the things I love. For always trusting me and believing in good. If you were any other way, I would not be able to say the things I say, or joke about the things I do. Morgan, No one will ever understand the bond we have. Thank you for being not only my sister, but my best friend, my unconditional support, my hero, and a voice of reason. Every time you are in pain, I ache. I can only imagine how hard this all must have been for you. From the little things like getting all of my school work during my significant absences, to talking me off the ledge on multiple occasions, I've never met someone with a heart as big as yours. Lindsey, For being the older sister, for getting up at the crack of dawn to get me coffee or food before school, for delivering things to the school whenever I asked, and going out of your way to make me happy. It cannot be easy being the one I always snap at after a bad day, but you never got angry with me or told me off. And to all my other family- for supporting from far and near. For the flowers, the food, and the showering of love, I am grateful beyond expression.

THE BEGINNING

How do you go from being perfectly healthy to being diagnosed with cancer? What do you do when everything takes a turn? How do you choose what to do and how to approach the situation? Those are only a few of the questions you begin to ask yourself when life throws a curveball at you.

An ordinary annual visit to my primary care physician left me with orders for blood work and an ultrasound of my neck. How? On March 4, 2013, my pediatrician felt an enlarged thyroid, a gland in the front of the neck, and decided to send me for blood work and an ultrasound. She promised it was nothing and she was just verifying her thoughts. Of course, with my anxious personality, I was rather irritated by the situation and just kept begging to push off what I felt would be a pointless waste of time. My mother scheduled my ultrasound for April 16th, 2013. I just brushed it off and hoped it would be forgotten. Well, it wasn't. A track meet was scheduled for the 16th, so the ultrasound had to be moved. March 28th was the new date. I went in for the blood work a couple of days before the ultrasound and my blood work came back normal, so you can only imagine how annoyed I was to be going in for what now seemed to be truly unnecessary. Little did I know that on that day, multiple masses would be discovered. I watched the radiologist take multiple photos and mark off certain measurements, but I thought that she was simply marking anatomy. When she was finished, she said she was going to check with the doctor and see if he wanted more scans. She came back and said I was good to go. That night after track practice, my mother told me that the doctors had found a large number of nodules spread throughout my neck. Even then, the chance of these nodules being malignant was slim. I still had not an ounce of doubt that this was simply protocol and I was one hundred percent healthy. I also found out that the doctor they checked in with before they released me from the ultrasound was my pediatrician.

1

From there a biopsy was ordered and I wasn't even given a say in when that appointment was. April 8, 2013, my father's birthday, I had the pleasure of being stuck with countless needles that I willingly watched be placed into my neck via the ultrasound machine. To top off that lovely day, I was not allowed to go to track practice which clearly didn't improve my attitude. We were told we would have the results in 2-3 days. I headed into school on Tuesday with no inklings on what my day would turn out to be.

I went into school with some pain in my neck and attended track practice after school. From track I went to a Student Council meeting where I was questioned about the band aid on my neck. Seeing as I was questioned by people I was somewhat close with, I shared the explanation for the band aid. Prior to this, maybe a handful of people knew I was having the biopsy done because I don't share things with people and I like to keep my personal life separate. I was questioned about results, which I was unaware had come in at that point. Once the meeting was over, I went home to get ready for dance, but when I got in the car, I heard the words "MacKenzie, we need to talk" come out of my mother's mouth. She didn't even need to say anything more, and I knew. Because of the way my schedule worked that day, others knew the results hours before I did, which at the time didn't phase me because I was too busy trying to wrap my head around the events of the last couple of days.

In complete disbelief, I asked her what I would have to do. She said the word that anyone who knows me would know that that single word would cut deeper than anything...SURGERY. To me surgery meant sitting out, recovery, medicine, doctors, hospitals, and everything I dislike all in a single swing.

I got out of the car, went inside and changed, and got ready to leave for dance, not even allowing myself to think about what had happened. I went to dance where I told my absolute best friend, the friend without whom I could never have made it through, what was happening. Being her emotional self, she cried and cried some more. After getting herself together, we went into class. A couple of hours later when dance was over, I went home to find out that pretty much my entire school had found out. I am probably one of the most private people, especially when it comes to personal things like this. I could not believe what my day turned into. That day went into the books as one of the worst days of my life and I could not bring myself to do my homework or anything else that night, which for me, type-A student, literally never happens. I decided to turn my phone on and see the damage. Countless texts, tweets, and well wishes, some from people I have never spoken a word to before, crammed the screen. I really appreciated everything, but I had kept everything about the situation between my family and a handful of friends, and now the entire school and beyond knew. All it took was an uneducated assumption, a single tweet, and a teenager with no filter on the mouth to spread this.

Just hours after I became aware of the diagnosis, while I was still in dance class, a parent without confirmation of my situation took it into her own hands and decided to tell the studio owners. Obviously I was not in the proper state of mind to share that information with them myself that particular night, however, when things settled down and it became necessary for them to be made aware, I would have shared the information. Not only was the diagnosis a fresh cut wound and I was trying to contain the outside knowledge of it, dance would not be one of the places I would choose for the information to be shared first. At the time of the diagnosis, I was a little disappointed in an action of one of the teachers revolving around the biopsy and my potential restrictions during class the following day. Eventually I would have gotten over that and the diagnosis would have been shared, but to this day, and probably forever, I will not be okay with this parent taking it into her own hands and sharing this private and personal issue with a studio of hundreds who come from all different parts of the area. After having this experience of betrayal, I am exceedingly careful with who I share such personal information with. Regardless of the fact that I didn't share this information with anyone other than family and a couple of very close friends, word got around and people didn't think before they talked about something they were hearing through the grapevine. I am phenomenal at holding grudges against people for actions like this. Like everyone. I have my differences with people. For some time after the diagnosis, people who I don't talk to, and people that I have my differences with, were acting all nice and fake. I cannot tolerate people like this; people who want to make themselves look good and start caring about another individual after something highly unfortunate happens to them. You can't possibly go from not caring about someone to instantly acting like you're their best friend and like you've been there for them for a great deal of time. Let's face it, it doesn't work like that. You can't all of sudden care so you can receive sympathy for what someone else is going through. I'll always struggle with how and who found out, but when all is said and done, you realize who genuinely cares and who will be there for you when you need someone to talk to. Needless to say, April 9, 2013 will forever be a memorable day, but not for a positive reason.

Just a couple of days after the diagnosis, doctors jumped right into things and began to take action. I would have loved for them to wait and take their time, but I should've known my wish was too far-fetched. Based on the ultrasound, it was unknown whether the cancer had spread to any lymph nodes. When I asked if I would need to have surgery immediately or if I could wait a couple of months...or maybe even years, I was told that if the MRI showed diseased lymph nodes, I would not be able to put off surgery. Chances were that if the disease had not spread to my lymph nodes, I would be able to wait a little bit longer, but not nearly the time I had hoped for.

March 11, 2013

On a rainy Thursday morning, I went in to the local hospital for an MRI. Like almost everyone else, I am not a fan of the loud and claustrophobic machines, but I didn't have much say in the matter. While being enclosed in the face mask, I had nothing to do but think. I just remember tears rolling down my face as I thought of what had transpired over the last couple of days.

Following the MRI, we were supposed to meet with a surgeon. That morning, radiology was all backed up and then my scan ended up being 2 hours late so we were late for my other appointment. As if I wasn't already upset and nervous enough, I was missing more school, and I wasn't being given confirmation on what at the time, felt like was going to determine my near future. On top of having to wait an additional two hours for my MRI, some of the scans didn't look clear, so they had to be repeated. When we finally got to the surgeon, we were unbelievably late. By this point, I was already more irritated than I had ever been in my sixteen years. The surgeon we met with was great; he was nice, knowledgeable, and relatively trustworthy. We had already been told we should probably make the switch to Children's Hospital in Boston, which we were highly considering, but we went ahead with meeting this surgeon so we had options on the table. I mean, we weren't prepared for any of this and the diagnosis was only 48 hours old and I was only three days post biopsy, we hadn't had much time to think about any of this before the appointments were just being scheduled for us and we weren't given a say in the times. One big issue stood out with this surgeon, he had never operated on a pediatric case because thyroid cancer in pediatric cases is so rare. With that knowledge, we were sold on switching hospitals. Fortunately, my pediatrician worked with Children's and got us an appointment with a surgeon she recommended for us. I was given a couple of weeks to relax and let everything sink in before my next appointment.

Sitting in the chair at the office listening to the surgeon, my attention drifted and I was no longer focusing on what he was saying, but rather how much of a turn my life had just taken. Being 16 and healthy one day to being 16 and having cancer another day wasn't easy for me to wrap my head around as it did not make any sense to me.

April 23, 2013

On April 23, 2013, my parents and I headed into Boston hoping for some good news. First we met with an ENT. When my mom was filling out the paperwork, one of the papers asked about the patient's history with a list of diseases. One of the options was "Cancer" and she wrote no. I remember saying, "then what are we doing here?" She hadn't accepted the diagnosis. Everything was happening so quickly and there wasn't any time to process it. The ENT stuck some tubes down my nose to see if the cancer had spread to my vocal chords. He didn't really have much to say, so we were confused. From that appointment, we then met with another surgeon. He was great! I mean, of course I hated my situation more than anything and I would have loved for it all to be a mistake, but that was unlikely. He seemed like the perfect fit; he had a great bedside manner, he was experienced in this field, and most importantly, he took the time to draw out the procedure for me and he explained it to me like I was the high school sophomore I was and not a fellow surgeon. He told me I could wait a little while, but surgery needed to be the beginning of June.

I needed to make it through States for track, competitions and recital for dance, and most importantly, as much of sophomore year as possible. To me, this meant a lot, whereas to other kids, they would have jumped at an opportunity to miss as much school as possible.

One problem, the MRI could not properly diagnose diseased lymph nodes, which means that test had been all a waste of time and unnecessary exposure to radiation. An ultrasound needed to be done for this part of the diagnosis. The surgeon and his team worked with Brigham and Women's to get me in that day for the ultrasound so we wouldn't have to make another trip. I headed over to Brigham and Women's for the ultrasound and we had to wait some more. I had planned on making it back to school for at least half of the day, but here we were, in Boston still waiting for another appointment. Chances of me making it back were slim.

I'll never forget my ultrasound tech from that day. He was easily one of the nicest and most sincere people I've had the pleasure of meeting. He too, had undergone a thyroidectomy. It was nice to hear his story and for him to offer his advice. After the ultrasound, I was finally allowed to leave and head home. I missed the entire day and part of practice because it took us two hours to get home after the countless hours in the hospital. On top of all of my actual homework and make up work for the day, the surgeon assigned me the task of picking a day for surgery. Clearly, this was worse than writing a 10 page paper for me.

Early May 2013

Some time after the ultrasound, my mom received a call from the surgeon confirming the cancer metastasizing to my lymph nodes. She was also told how many lymph nodes needed to be removed. For some reason, I was never made aware of this phone call. Instead I found out about it maybe 10 days before surgery when I was waiting in line at Subway when the topic came up.

After the ultrasounds and all of the testing, I started to notice a couple of rock like sticks in my neck which I then realized were diseased lymph nodes. There was one that was really noticeable to me because it juts out of my neck slightly. Back in maybe November or around that time, I remember feeling this prominent lymph node on the left side of my neck, but at the time, I figured it was just a part of my neck structure. Once I realized this, I grew mad at myself because I just kept thinking what would have been different if it was caught earlier, and in my case, I was the only one who knew about this structure in my neck, so it is on me. When I told my mom about this she questioned why I would even begin to blame myself. She didn't understand why I was going to kick myself because one day I felt a weird bulge in my neck and I didn't think it was an issue that warranted a trip to the doctor. I laid off of blaming myself a little bit, but I just didn't understand how I didn't think anything of it. Over time, I thought to myself; who would think that a structure like this in my neck would later be diagnosed as cancer and I had no idea the whole time. Of course, I would never *want* to go to the doctor so I obviously wouldn't mention anything that had potential to hand me a doctor's appointment. Every once in a while I'll think about how things could've been if I had caught this earlier, but I really need to stop blaming my ignorance for the severity of my case.

Here's the thing, to escape this predicament is impossible. There isn't anything myself or anyone else could've done to prevent this situation. Going back in time wouldn't do anything, it would eventually happen, but fast forwarding also wouldn't do anything because the operation is over and done with. I don't have a thyroid anymore and I'm tied to my endocrinologist, bloodwork, medicine, and the whole package for the rest of my life. Nothing can or will ever change that. I'll never be the person I was before: physically or mentally. I'll never be able to do everything I could before surgery; I'll always have to accept my limitations and move on, not matter how difficult it is. I just have to be thankful that the disease was caught early enough that there were things that could be done and that I'm still here today.

The night of my first appointment at Children's, I sat down with all of my calendars and tried to see what I had to work with. June 7th seemed like it was the latest the surgeon would allow, but the earliest I was "available." June 7th it was. My mom called the next morning to schedule, but radiology unfortunately couldn't be there that day so the 6th was the day. I let everything sink in before I made anyone aware of the date.

Mid May 2013

Under the impression that all my teachers had heard about the situation, I didn't feel the need to talk to them about it. Some time in the middle of May, I went to guidance to inform them of the situation and my upcoming absence. My guidance counselor handled the situation with respect and confidentiality. Somehow the administration found out about it the same day as me, but they kept it to themselves. She said that she had known, but she was waiting for me to come talk to her instead of her bringing it up. Once I talked to her, she emailed my teachers to inform them of my year ending earlier. She did not tell them why or anything, just that I would be leaving early. Eventually, I made my rounds with my teachers where they did ask questions and I didn't want to lie. I thought that they knew, but I was mistaken.

Each day after school, I would conquer talking with one of my teachers. Knowing that they would most likely have questions, I needed to break it up this way because I could only handle so much in a single day. I went to the teachers I figured would be harder for me to tell first, and finished with the ones I figured would be easier. All of them had a similar reaction and offered the same advice, however they all seemed to have a different way of expressing their responses. While some teachers asked far more questions than I would have liked and made me feel awkward and uncomfortable, others expressed the same level of concern but respected my privacy in doing so.

After speaking to seven teachers, extracurricular advisors, and everyone else who needed to be informed, I had my speech mastered. Oddly, each time got harder to say because it made it like I was drilling it into my head because I hadn't yet accepted it.

In contrast to how the news spread to the studio, the staff at school who knew kept it to themselves and let me handle it on my own terms. Maybe this had something to do with respect or maybe it had something to do with the rules they must follow; either way, I accepted the varying ways people handled the situation and moved on.

June 3, 2013

On June 3, 2013, I headed into Boston for my pre-op appointment. The hospital seemed to have a much darker overtone to it this time, which I'm going to chalk up to my crushed hopes of this falling through or there being other options. Children's Hospital is a brutal place. You see so many things you wish you never saw. Kids who don't have a chance to do everything you've gotten to do. Parents barely holding on. You never realize how lucky you are. There is always someone worse off than you; never forget that.

I was in the room with a fish tank that sent me back to my childhood where everything was simple and all was good in the world. After seeing a handful of doctors, answering a million questions, waiting around, we went to the lab and then to school. On this day, having a handful of different types of doctors talk to me about their role in the surgery made me recognize that this was really going to happen. At one point, I said to my mom, "can they just do the surgery now?" Of course I didn't actually want it done, but I knew there was no way out so just getting it done when I was already there would've just prevented all of the anxiety I knew I would have just three days later. With 72 hours left before the surgery, I had lots of time to ponder details about the surgery and overwhelm myself with all of the what if's. Even knowing as many details about the surgery and processing all of this, I still felt so unprepared.

June 5, 2013

As the big day approached, my nerves were getting the best of me. I was finding it extremely hard to focus on school and time felt like it was flying by and dragging on at the same time. It was strange waking up knowing that it was going to be my last day of sophomore year, yet it wasn't actually the last day of school. The whole day is a blur and I don't think I paid attention in any of my classes. My friends, teachers, and administration knew that it was my last day and it was the weirdest feeling. For everyone else, it was a typical day. I had a lot of things I needed to wrap up after school and I needed to make sure everything was all set. Fortunately track was over because by the end of the day, I had had it with everything. My patience was very thin and the only thing on my mind was finding out what time surgery was. At 3 O'clock we could call in and get the time. I got in the car and that was the first thing I did. I got really anxious, and when the clock struck 3 I felt my stomach drop and my heart beat at an increasing rate. As the phone rang, it felt like it took forever for them to pick up and let us know. When they finally did, they said 7:30 A.M. which is the first spot. With this slot, I knew I wouldn't get pushed off because my surgeon wouldn't get tied up in another surgery. Also, with the 7:30 slot, I figured I would be done no later than noon time and I would be able to go home first thing Friday morning. Just 24 hours later, my prediction would prove totally incorrect. One hurdle had been cleared, but the biggest still lay ahead. The night dragged on. I didn't have any homework to do and I had no distraction. I procrastinated on packing my bag because I didn't want it to become that real. I didn't know what to do with myself and that alone was the worst possible thing that could've happened. When it was finally time, I headed to bed but not before enjoying my last comfortable shower for a long time and taking in the last time I'd ever see my neck in the same light. I knew I would hardly sleep but it was worth a shot.

June 6, 2013

June 6, 2013 came a lot faster than I ever anticipated. I made it through the torture of dancing three recitals in one weekend, running the Larry Olsen 5K, finishing the track season, doing as much school work as possible and wrapping up most of the loose ends. The only thing left staring me in the face was the thing I have dreaded more than anything else... The one thing I cringed at every time I looked at the calendar... SURGERY. Not only was the day going to be one of the hardest days of my life, but I could only imagine how my family would do. My mother and father had been through this more than ten times with my two sisters. My older sister had had countless ear and throat surgeries in her younger years, and my twin had been in the operating room twice in the last three years. To be honest, I have no idea how they held it together for this long. As soon as it seemed like we were going to catch a break, something else happened.

10

That morning, we packed up and headed into Boston. It was an exceedingly dismal morning dark, cold, and rainy. I sat in the backseat with a nice furry blanket covering me and with my head resting on my zebra print body pillow. During my pre-op appointment I had asked the nurse practitioner 2 things: one, could I change into my own clothes when I got to my room, and two, could I bring my own pillow and blanket. To me, those were two of the things that were of top priority.

We walked into the hospital and went to check in. Obviously no one was happy to be there, parents or patients, how could you be? Each surgery carries with it its own risks and dangers, some more severe than others. Parents think the worst, even when they act all positive for their kids. As a teenager, I can only imagine what it is like to be the parent of a sick child and how they have to be so strong and act all positive. It's really got to take a toll on them.

I was given a pregnancy test, which really didn't sit well with me. Yeah, the doctors have to cover all the bases so nothing can get them in trouble, but at the expense of the patient. I could promise you I was not pregnant, but it is my word against potential lawsuits. Whatever.

A nurse came and took me to my pre-op room. Everything was so dark and you could tell that was one of the roughest floors in the building. Some parents could be saying goodbye to their children for the last time and not even know it. All of the rooms were curtained off and very small. I changed into the god awful gown and got some nice socks and pants...just kidding-- they're just as bad as the gown. Almost everyone who was going to be in on my surgery came in one by one to take care of their business. A little girl was across the way from me. She was playing with the cup and doing the famous cup song that had grown in popularity since the release of Pitch Perfect, too young to realize what's going on. Her innocence elicited a slight positivity in me. If she could be so young and so strong, I could hold myself together too. When the anesthesiologist came in, he informed us that I may have a Catheter due to the length of the operation, which at the time was estimated at 4 hours. I was livid; feeling like this was just one more form of violation.

My surgeon was the last to arrive. He brought with him the dreaded consent form that carried my last bit of hope of escaping surgery. There was maybe a .05% chance I would manage to leave the hospital right then, but I never gave up that hope. He read me and my parents the form. One box that stood out to me was the alternatives; everything else was kind of a blur because I was not paying 100% attention. When he read off the alternatives box, he said, "NONE. You go to any hospital and they're going to want to take your thyroid out." He handed me a pen to sign, not that my signature really mattered. I signed it because that was my only option and handed it to my mom. Once that pen hit the paper, I knew that was it. It was actually happening. The anesthesiologist came in and put an IV in my right forearm. The whole team followed him and they gave me a medicine to help me relax. I said goodbye to my parents and tears started pouring down my face. I knew I would survive, I trusted my surgeon with my life, but I was still in disbelief and I really just wanted this to be a joke. I just stared at the ceiling the whole way to the operating room wondering what the next couple hours would be like. Once we entered the operating room, it was nothing like what I had pictured. It was dark and cold, a very unwelcoming place. I transferred to a metal table. A couple of pillows were placed under my knees. I can't remember everything from that point on, probably a good thing. A mask was placed over my mouth and they told me to relax and take a breath. It seemed like it was forever before I went out.

I woke up in a room I really can't describe as I was heavily under the influence of several drugs. I remember being in tears. Not because my neck hurt, but because my butt hurt. I have an extremely bony and muscular butt and being under, on a metal table for as long as I was, did not help my cause. I thought it was around noon, but it was almost 5 o'clock.

I can't even remember initially waking up, but my mom has told me stories. I asked over and over again if I had a catheter; I guess that was the only thing I really cared about. Because of the pain, the nurses gave me morphine which can make you itchy. My mom told me that I kept asking her to itch my nose and I kept moving her finger because she wasn't doing a good enough job. I also asked the nurse for ice...who does that? One thing I do remember is begging for ice chips. As far as I know, my neck wasn't bothering me one bit! Before surgery, one of my biggest minor concerns was what I was going to say when I came out of the anesthesia. I told my mom she was going to have to duct tape my mouth shut because chances were, I was going to say things I shouldn't.

A couple hours after surgery, I was moved upstairs to my room. I can't even remember the trip from recovery to my room. As they were wheeling me into my room, they told me I got the luxury suite because one of the sides was all windows, but at that point, I didn't care. The only thing I cared about what getting out of that place. I had cords and wires everywhere and I was not happy about it at all. I had two blood pressure cuffs on my ankles and I was just so uncomfortable and irritated that I had a meltdown. The nurse was nice enough to remove these cuffs and allow me to put my own shorts on.

I told my parents that I was fine and that they could leave and go grab something to eat. I was going to turn my phone on and respond to people and take care of a call I was supposed to make. When I turned my phone on I had about 150 text messages and countless twitter and Instagram notifications. I was so dizzy and incapable of focusing. I couldn't concentrate on anything I was doing. Looking at the screen was a challenge, never mind responding to people. I was too disoriented. There were a couple of people who I knew I needed to talk to so I made that a priority. I started to text my best friend but it was too difficult so I decided to call her instead. Weeks later I found out what I was saying and thank god I said it to her and not someone else. I guess I was more confident in my abilities than I should have been. I made the second phone call and then I called it quits, or at least I thought. Weeks later when I was going through my phone, I found a bunch of conversations I didn't know I had had. My sister called me so I did talk to her. She made plans to FaceTime me later that night. I must have dozed off because when I woke up, my parents were back in my room. Before I went to sleep, I facetimed with Morgan where she showed me the gifts I received from STUCO[1] Eboard and a couple of friends. I don't remember this conversation at all and when I finally did get home, I had no idea what these gifts were, or who they were from.

Right after arriving in my room, there was a shift change. I only had the transport nurse and my floor nurse for a little while. I was too under the influence to have an accurate judgement of what was going on around me.

---

[1] Student Council Executive Board

June 7, 2013

The first night was a rough one. Every couple of minutes there was someone coming in to check my vitals or to give me one of my medicines. The pain started to kick in too. The sound on my heart monitor was shut off because my heart rate was so low that I was setting it off all night.

The next day I was expecting to be released. They took my morning labs and we waited for the results. I hadn't eaten or drunk anything nor did I want to. The bearer of bad news came in and told me that my calcium was too low for me to be discharged so of course, I had yet another meltdown. Like I thought my tears would make them feel bad and discharge me... come on, that's crazy.

I was up pretty early that morning and I hadn't slept that well. I was supposed to be attending an Eboard meeting before school that morning, but obviously that wasn't going to happen. I facetimed into the meeting so I wouldn't miss too much. I muted the phone and turned the camera around because I didn't want anyone to see me. I can't remember a single thing that was discussed. At this point I wasn't too distraught as there were still not results from the labs yet.

Once my labs were drawn, I was there to witness yet another shift change. To my surprise, the same floor nurse from my arrival in recovery was back. Only this time, she would learn how awful of a patient I am.

Throughout that day, too many people to count were in and out. I did quite a bit of sleeping. I was extremely uncomfortable and upset. One endocrinologist came in and asked me and my mom some questions. Questions I really had no desire to be answering. By this point in June, I was already pretty tan. Due to some thyroid issues causing darker pigmentation of the skin, he questioned if I was always this tan. Yes, I am very dark! He came back later with a group of people, and again, asked these awful questions. He even asked me to show him my tan lines so he could confirm the response. Awkward. Because I wasn't being discharged, Morgan got dismissed from school and came to the hospital to see me.

I can't say that at any point when I was in the hospital that I was in pain. I knew I was far too uncomfortable for my liking, but I don't know if I was trying to convince myself that I wasn't in pain and that I was only uncomfortable. I knew going into surgery, taking medicine was going to be the biggest challenge for me. I wanted to do it drug free, but there was not a chance of that happening. I'm the kid who can't even bring myself to take Advil or Motrin. I don't know exactly why, but people assume it's because of the fear of addiction, but to be honest, I don't even think that part crossed my mind. There was just something about pain relievers and all forms of medicine that I just didn't like.

I convinced myself I wasn't in pain and hadn't had pain meds since that morning. At this point I was so beyond the point of being uncomfortable that I was having meltdowns every couple minutes. I still had not eaten anything besides a couple of Popsicles and sips of ginger ale. Because I was so uncomfortable my body reacted with legs shaking uncontrollably, so the nurses were trying to hold them down and they couldn't.

Low calcium is common after a thyroidectomy, and it can lead to heart attacks and seizures. Because my calcium levels were low that morning and I was unable to go home, nurses were concerned my calcium dipped even lower and I was going to slip into a seizure at any moment. I distinctly remember my nurse yelling out my door, "We have a post op butterfly in here. Drawing her labs early. Page surgery!" That was pretty concerning. I didn't know what was going on. The nurse came in to take my blood and my veins had collapsed and she couldn't get any blood. I say that she went "fishing" in my left arm to find a vein, which by the way left a lovely bruise. She then tried to draw from both of my IV's, but that didn't work. So she tried my right arm. After a couple of minutes, she finally got it. I don't have an issue with getting blood taken, as long as I'm not watching. Needles don't scare me and they don't cause me any discomfort, but looking at the blood just creeps me out so I just don't watch. This experience however, was rather traumatizing. I was in tears, not only because it was painful but because I was just so overwhelmed and scared. I like to call this whole ordeal, episode one. After my labs were drawn, I was forced to eat. My sister and dad went across the street to Bertucci's so get me something easy to eat. Being my stubborn self, I wanted nothing to do with the food. I didn't have a choice. Before they got back, I got up to go to the bathroom. This particular nurse was the nurse I had when I first got moved upstairs until her shift ended. I really liked her so when she came back on Friday morning I was happy, but I did not anticipate having to spend the day. She would not let me do anything myself. I didn't need an escort to the bathroom. I'm 16 years old; I've been doing this forever. She told me she was my worst nightmare; my second mother, and my nurse. That is a deadly combination.

During the day, the child life specialist came in to offer me things to do because it is really boring just sitting there in a hospital bed, but since I felt stranger than I ever had and I couldn't move my head, focus or stay awake for longer than an hour, I was just not in a good place and I don't think anything could have changed that. The hospital had four tickets to Sunday's Red Sox game. They were really good seats and they offered them to me. I figured by Sunday I would be all set and it was a great opportunity! The Bruins had a game on Friday night so I was looking forward to watching it, thought I would much rather have been in the comfort of my own home. I made a comment about how cool it would've been to go to the Bruins game that night. The nurse agreed and she said that of course I would've had to take a nurse with me, just so she could come! It wouldn't have mattered how much pain I was in or how uncomfortable I was, I would've been there!

The day went by pretty slowly and episode one had exhausted me. My surgeon came up that night when Morgan was in my bed with me. He told me I gave him a run for his money! Now he's been doing this for quite some time, so that's an accomplishment. He also told me he heard about the episode and he said that I needed to take my pain medicine; now was not the time to be a hero. He left and then my dad and sister left. It was just me and my mom. The shift changed for another night and my nurse, otherwise known as my worst nightmare, was leaving for the night. She was easily one of my favorite staff members at Children's. She made my stay more comforting and added some relief to the not so cheery hospital. It's always interesting to see who the new staff is and we got to witness quite a few shift changes. My next nurse was just as good as the others fortunately. Nothing is worse than a nurse who does not allow you to sleep.

June 8, 2013

When I woke up for good that morning the nurse came in with my medicine. Just minutes after taking the pain meds I got really nauseous and started to gag. I had nothing in my stomach. I was so concerned that

I was going to rip through my stitches. She hooked me back up to my IV and gave me anti-nausea medicine. The medicine didn't seem to help me at all, but that could've been because something happened with the IV bag and there was liquid all over my pillow and all down my arm and we are not sure where it came from, but it could also be because of deathly fear of nausea and vomit. I call this episode two. After a while the doctors came in and said that my calcium was good enough to be discharged. I was cleared by endocrinology to go home, but because of my reaction to my pain meds, surgery didn't want to send me home. They wanted to monitor me through at least one more round of medicine. After a while we gave up and they decided to let me go home! I didn't plan on taking the pain meds anyways so it didn't matter. My dad headed into Boston to pick us up. The nurse came in with countless prescriptions--I don't even know what they were for. I was finally removed from my monitors and allowed to put my own clothes on. I didn't feel well at all, but I just wanted to be in the comfort of my own home. I hated staying in the hospital and being locked up inside. I changed and got ready to leave. I was put in a wheelchair and we made our way downstairs. As we were leaving, it was all new territory of the hospital for me. If I hadn't been so disoriented when they took me up days before, chances are I would have had a clue where we were going. My dad pulled the car around and I got in and tried to make myself as comfortable as possible. I had a two hour drive ahead of me. We stopped at Dunkin Donuts so my parents could force me to drink something. After that we hit the road and made our way home.

I was still in good shape so we stopped at CVS to get my prescriptions filled. The pharmacy didn't have one of the medicines I needed. After about an hour of waiting in the car, I needed to be home. I was about to have another meltdown and I needed to lie down. My dad went in and got my mom and we finally went home.

Walking through the doors of the house was the best feeling. It was sort of a milestone. A piece of the puzzle was solved and I was one step closer to being cancer free. I went upstairs and sat on the couch. There were flowers everywhere and some special ones from my sisters. They were my favorite flowers in the thyroid cancer colors. I love photography and flowers are one of the main things I take pictures of. I couldn't wait to get my camera out and take pictures! There were also balloons and gifts all over the place. I really hate attention, but it meant a lot to see how many people cared. I was still not feeling great. I got my stuff all set up on the couch in the living room and tried to take a nap.

My best friend and second mother showed up at my house to surprise me. I was thrilled to see her. Ariana and her family were my biggest supporters through this point. They were so kind and respectful and I'm so lucky I had the pleasure of meeting them. The brought over meals and gifts. Having them over was a big distraction from how crappy I felt and I was able to forget as much as it was possible to forget, what was going on. After they left my final round of meds of the day came in. I had started this new thing where every time the calcium carbonate came near me, I would groan and whine. Calcium carbonate is the worst thing I have ever smelt or tasted in my life. I couldn't stand the thought of it. I still cringe every time I think about it. Once the parade of medicine was over, I headed up to my parents' room where I was going to be sleeping on their couch for a little while.

- -

I am so lucky that I had the experience with the hospital that I did. Switching hospitals was worth it. The opportunities and care that Children's Hospital in Boston offers is worth the drive. The atmosphere of the hospital is vastly different than that of any other hospital I have been in. Perhaps because of the fact that they are a hospital specifically dedicated to treating children, everyone who works there has a positive attitude and they're always looking to improve your stay and ease the suffering of the families who may need it.

- -

June 9, 2013

I woke up a couple of times throughout the night to take some Motrin, but overall it was the best night yet. I woke up pretty early that morning feeling nauseous. After a minor panic attack, I relocated to the couch downstairs. The medicine truck had arrived for delivery. Each dose of calcium got worse and worse. All of the other meds were fine. I was glued to the couch for a while so it was time to catch up on all of the television I never watched because I was too busy. The effects of the breathing tube from surgery were starting to kick in. I had so much mucus in my throat but I couldn't cough, and swallowing wasn't working. I kept choking and at points, I couldn't breathe. I kept drinking to try and get it to move. I let out a tiny cough to try and move it and everything seemed to calm down for a little bit. My cousins came over to see me and they were all scared of my bandages, I mean it is pretty scary for kids under five. Then the second half of this fiasco came. This time, only worse. I could not breathe and I couldn't get the mucus to move. My mom called the hospital and they were going to check with the doctors to see what to do. They called back a little while later while I was still struggling to breathe and move this mucus. Finally it just moved and I was hoping that there wouldn't be a phase three. I like to call this episode three.

Two of my aunts came over later and they brought food with them, another tactic to get me to eat.

My mother won the battle and I had food for the first time since Wednesday. I was surprised at how much of a challenge swallowing was. I had some discomfort with swallowing in the hospital but nothing too bad. After eating, I was completely exhausted and I went back into the living room to rest. For the rest of the day things calmed down and I was able to relax with minor discomfort.

- -

After coming home from the hospital and when I finally had my drugless senses back, it was important to me to know everything that happened to me. I'm sure my family got annoyed with me, but it was totally worth it. Being someone who thoroughly relied on having control of myself and my actions, the operating room put me in an inevitable state of vulnerability. I was aware that my body would be invaded in ways I wished it never would, but I also understand that the only way to get rid of the cancer was to be put in that very state of no control I dreaded my entire life. I needed to know every detail that they knew from the events that took place in the operating room and recovery, prior to my return to awareness.

My parents told me about their meeting with my surgeon while they were waiting to see me in recovery and they were recalling how exhausted he looked. He had said that I had been a tough one and how surprised he was with the progression of the disease and how solid my thyroid and lymph nodes were. And for some reason, I think it's somewhat comical... Go Big or Go Home? Guess I went big and made him work. It was also evident that the doctors and nurses don't disclose any information they're not required to. I wish I could remember everything that happened or that I was told, but because of the medicines and inability to move around, I can't remember all of the little details about the experience. No matter how much time passes, I will always be frustrated that I can't remember every miniscule detail about the experience.

RELATIONSHIPS DURING CANCER

Through the diagnosis and surgery, I was in a decent relationship. I knew it was going to be tough and I knew my reaction would create tension everywhere. The last thing I wanted was a pity card. Now, knowing what happened, I'm almost positive he stayed with me because he didn't want to look bad for leaving me when I was sick. I had a feeling things were going to go downhill. I gave him a get out of jail free card around 20 times. He refused to take it. At this point in life, not many teenage boys are capable of handling something like this, and it's not expected that they should. However, if you don't bail before and you make promises, you should never break that promise. I did everything in my power to stay strong and not rely on anyone. I tried my best to inform him first so he wouldn't get upset. As surgery got closer, I could tell he was lacking. I didn't expect much from him and I was nowhere near a controlling girlfriend. We were both extremely busy with school and sports and everything else which was good for me because I used that as my escape. The night before surgery I did expect him to talk to me and be supportive, but once again, he was carrying on with his shenanigans again. Just before I went to bed, he finally texted me. I talked with him for a little bit and then attempted to sleep. He told me "If I'm not the first one you talk to when you wake up, I'm going to be pissed." It's like I was actually scared because the first thing I did when I was stable enough, was call him. I was so concerned about him getting mad at me that that was my biggest fear. I didn't hear too much from him when I was in the hospital. When I got home, he made no effort to talk to me or come and see me. On Saturday, I was having a really bad day and I hadn't talked to him so I texted him. His response was, "I would love to talk, but I'm at a graduation party." I understand he's busy, but then he shouldn't have said, "No matter when, I'll be here to talk. "Clearly that was a lie. School was winding down at this point and there wasn't a lot left to be done. He never made an effort to see me, and then he left for vacation without even talking to me. I saw some twitter drama and I quickly grew irritated. For months, I had let him walk all over me. I had given him the benefit of the doubt and I only looked for the good and forgave for the bad. I looked past every single thing that he had done and stood by his side. Never once on vacation did he text just to talk or anything, which I didn't expect, but he decided to text me when he had a question about my sister. OK, that's cool. I just stopped responding to him and left him to be alone on vacation with his family. He begged and begged to talk on the phone, so I gave in and called him. I say what happened wasn't at all what I was expecting, but I sort of knew it was coming. I had too much to deal with and I didn't need to be associated with someone like that. No matter what I did, it wasn't good enough and it was always his way or the highway. Now he may see things differently, but take it as it is, things were ugly. Not just because the relationship was over, but more so because of the things he said that night, I lost all respect. I didn't want to make him look bad so I didn't share anything. Once again, I thought about him before I thought about myself. It's not about who broke up with whom or anything like that. At this point, I should've done what was best for me and I shouldn't have allowed him to walk all over me. Moral of the story, don't wait things out and pretend everything in the end will be ok. Almost no one is strong enough to handle this, no matter how many times they promise they'll be there for you. It's not worth the added stress and aggravation the shenanigans cause. I don't regret this because it forced me to accept people for who they are, as well as to free yourself from anything that is going to bring you down, especially when you are squaring up with adversity.

After the final dose of medicine for the day, I headed to bed. I slept OK that night. I was in much more discomfort than I had been, yet I still refused to resort to the prescription pain meds.

June 10, 2013

I had to get up the next morning and go get labs done to monitor my calcium and thyroid levels. I looked pretty beat up, but at this point, I don't think I really cared. My desire to look halfway decent when I was out in public didn't even come near my desire for this whole medical issue to end.

The morning came faster than I would have liked, but I got up and got ready to bring Morgan to school and go get labs drawn. When we pulled up to the school, out of habit I got ready to get out. I really didn't want to go to school, but also didn't want to be in my situation. I really don't enjoy school, so I couldn't tell you why I wanted to get out. I never really missed school so one would think that this would be great; no school, extended summer, no finals...good joke, I'd take all of that over the disease and its loyal followers.

Instantly after surgery, I figured I would be able to tackle some STUCO work and other things I needed to take care of. I was sorely mistaken. I had promised an email immediately after, but I completely forgot for a couple of days. I kept trying to push myself to get my work done, but everything about it seemed impossible. Frustration was not making the work do itself, so I just added pointless stress to a body that was already struggling to heal. Word to the wise: give yourself time, let your body heal. You will only set yourself further back if you try to be a hero.

On Monday night I had a couple of visitors. I had become very close with some of the seniors and they were really big supporters. They brought me candy and gifts. They were great at distracting me and they were great for some good laughs. I knew it would be a challenge to see them leave in just a few short months.

With all the tough things going on, it didn't take much to make me happy. Once the results of the labs came in, I was allowed to cut my calcium carbonate doses in half. Typically, no one would get excited about that, but under the circumstances that was pretty great news.

Throughout the course of the week there were a great number of visitors. It was tough because all of my friends were still in school so I was bored. I'm not good at being bored because I never have time and I'm always running from place to place without time to even think. Thinking and overthinking are two big issues for me. With all this time on my hands (even though I had things to be doing), all I did was think about absolutely everything about my life and activities. In between all of this thinking, I stressed about the things that weren't getting done, but really needed to.

Around the middle of June, the doctors called with the pathology reports. Nothing other than what we expected. The tumor that was found on my trachea was sent to be tested and that too came back malignant. More than twenty lymph nodes were removed and tested, all of which came back positive. A piece of tissue from the left side of my neck was removed and tested as well. We didn't expect anything different from the results, but it would've been nice if it was all a mistake. But, even if it was all a mistake, I still went through the surgery and everything else so not much would change.

June 18, 2013

Dance has been a part of my life since the age of three. I was given the opportunity to grow and be pushed to new lengths by being put in dances with kids much older than I at the time. Unfortunately, this upset some parents and made me feel uncomfortable. I couldn't control how other people felt so I made it my goal to just take advantage of the opportunities that I was given and be the best that I could be. Because I have the ability to read people, I could see that these opportunities had upset others and I could sense who was upset. For years, this didn't change but I just learned who I could and couldn't trust as well as who the situation irritated and just avoided conflict with them. I wasn't the one making the groups and placing people in their numbers for the year so I couldn't take responsibility.

I decided to take a trip into the studio to visit with my friends and the teachers. In all honesty, it may have put me in a worse place because I didn't need to see the fake love and support from the people I know didn't care. For weeks I had been teetering on whether or not to dance again. A handful of people had sucked the fun out of it for me and I only had one person who really cared about me. I have had numerous issues with teachers and parents so everything was a struggle. I've tried to look at the pros and cons of sticking with it and I always end up with more negatives. But it always comes back to the thought of quitting after I've spent so much time and energy and my parents have spent so much money. I've held on for so long through the politics and drama, but it just doesn't seem worth it anymore. I know I don't want to dance in college, but I still don't want to give it up for my last two years. I know physically my body can't handle it at the current time, but down the road it may. I'm already upset with the restrictions my body has given itself and I've had a hard time accepting my limits, so I feel like going into the studio and trying to do everything I could do before and realizing I can't would cause me even more issues.

- -

THE ACT OF ACCEPTING

Accepting is easily the worst part of recovery; it's not the pain or the blood or the gory appearance. Everyone who faces cancer accepts their diagnosis at different times and with different approaches. It took me far longer than I'd like to admit for me to accept my diagnosis. At the time of my diagnosis, I felt like superwoman. I could last days without sleep and I could manage a schedule with far more than anyone should. I ran from one activity to another and never got tired. I never got sick and never missed school. I was content with my physical capabilities. I had the ability to lift people who weighed more than me and I had a toned body that granted me the ability to be successful in my sports. Coming to terms with my diagnosis meant that I would need to recognize that I no longer fit into the category of normal. However, looking back, I do wish that I came to terms earlier because I spent far too long pretending I was still normal and I didn't have cancer. In doing this, I repressed all emotions associated with it and when the time came, everything happened all at once. I'll never accept what I went through as a setback and I'll always pretend it's my fault for one reason or another or that I'm just not working hard enough.

SACRIFICE

Sacrifice has also been a big part of recovery. I always try to fit everything in so I'm not letting anyone down. Two weeks after surgery I was supposed to head down to the Cape with Eboard for leadership training and I was really looking forward to being outside and to some freedom from the disease, but it just wasn't a good idea. I still was only feeling a mere 50%, I was still on medicine, I couldn't be exposed to the sun for too long, and I couldn't hold my neck up. To my disappointment, my parents and my doctors decided it would be best if I didn't attend, for fear of a larger setback. It seemed like every day, there was something I had to sacrifice because of the disease or recovery.

Sometimes these sacrifices may come at times when you least expect them. They come in all different sizes and there's no way of predicting their size and arrival. As I got further into my battle, the sacrifices grew and became more frequent. From outpatient doctor's appointments to long absences from school, every corner I turned, something had to give. I couldn't do everything I wanted to; there just wasn't enough time and my body certainly couldn't handle everything it used to. I would be the one to turn in for the night because I was exhausted at 9 P.M. while everyone else my age was out having a great time. Maybe these sacrifices were a way of telling me that I needed to relax and lighten my load in order to enjoy the most important things, and to do these things well.

With any chronic illness, the sacrifices never end. Even when you're doing well and almost healthy, you can never escape the disease. There will always some type of physical or emotional reminder that holds you back from feeling normal again. Your life will be forever altered, but it's what you make of it and how you spin the negatives to positives that determine your happiness.

- -

June 29, 2013

I have always fallen back on running, field hockey, and dance to get me through the rough times. A big college recruiting tournament was coming up at Bentley University and my club team was participating. No matter how far from "ready" I was to play, I needed to. Just a couple of hours to get rid of some of the stress. Chances were, I wasn't going to cause myself any more pain, so what was the harm? It didn't take a lot to convince my mom to let me play. She understood it was what I needed and she knew Morgan would be right there to tell me to stop. She agreed to let me play.

I got up early that morning really excited to play. As I was getting ready, I felt the need to sneeze. Nothing could ruin my day so for the first time since surgery, I allowed myself to sneeze. The relief was nothing compared to the pain. It felt so good, yet so painful. I got ready and headed off to play. I'm not sure if I've ever been so excited to play before. I hadn't run or done any activity so I knew I was in horrible shape. I had just met with the surgeon and I begged him to clear me. I was ready.

I didn't play my best, and as much as I was upset at myself for that, I should've never expected that after a month of no activity and a major operation, that I would be able to play 100%. During one of our last games, I took a stick to the neck where the smaller incision was located. I'm not going to say it was pleasant, but it WAS NOT going to get in the way of me playing.

I knew that once the adrenaline wore off, all the pain would kick in and I would pay for my desires. It meant the world to be put on the field again. Even if it wasn't my best, I gave it all I had at the time and I guess that's all that matters. For the next few days, I knew I needed to take it easy and recover from the weekend.

End of June 2013

On a positive note, my calcium was improving and my dose kept decreasing. Not having to fill my body with medicine at all points of the day was a big step in the right direction.

Towards the end of June, it was time to meet with my endocrinologist in Boston. I never wanted to see that hospital again, but I felt like I could never escape it. I already had a little bit of knowledge about the Radioactive Iodine treatment that I was going to be receiving shortly and just based on that, I knew I wanted absolutely nothing to do with it. The doctor discussed the treatment and everything it entailed. She made a detailed schedule and explained the whole process. The body needs to be strong to handle this treatment so she wanted me to wait longer than eight weeks. Eight weeks from surgery brought me out to the beginning of August and that was pushing it time wise. School would be starting and field hockey would be at the top of my list. I didn't have time. Maybe I thought that if I kept finding an excuse not to have the treatment, everyone would just forget and we could all move on. Face the facts, this will not be forgotten and I will have the treatment no matter what, there was no way around it. I was told that the Radioactive Iodine treatment was much worse than surgery. I had to settle for the last week of July and the first week of August. The whole process takes around a month not including recovery. The starting date would be July 12th and I would receive the actual iodine on August 2nd. I went home stressed and upset. If I thought I didn't want to this before, this appointment made me really hate the idea of going forward. Good thing I'm not 18 and I don't have a say in these decisions.

A couple of days after meeting with the endocrinologist, I was on my way back into Boston for a follow up with my surgeon. I was still covered in steri strips so he couldn't get a good look at the incision itself, but good enough to let me start physical activity at a minimal amount. He wanted to see me again so he could check the incisions. Leaving the steri strips on would help the scars heal nicer so I never peeled them off no matter how annoying they were. Being uncomfortable now was much more worth it than an ugly scar.

I felt as though every day I would wake up after a horrible night's sleep and I'd have to go have labs done. As if I didn't hate Children's Hospital enough, I couldn't escape Milford hospital either. If it wasn't one thing, it was always another. I was still in pain and at this point I was too fed up with it to function. I was always having a meltdown of some sort. Each day seemed to get worse and worse. It was never a complete day without some kind of bad news.

July 2, 2013

I had started my freshman year at a new school as a school choice student. Due to budget circumstances, it was in our best interest to change schools. The big picture has always been college and with accreditation on the line, it was necessary. I have remained very close to a couple of girls from my old school. Every once in a while we will all get together and hang out. We don't talk every day or see each other all the time, but they are a huge support system. I tried to keep the situation private, but that only lasted for about an hour, and even then, I didn't reach out to anyone and tell them; they all found out through social media or through communication with other people. With the diagnosis out of the bag, they all became aware. I thought the news had been contained to dance and school, but quickly local schools found out. My attempt at keeping the diagnosis under the radar had failed. They all sent me texts informing me that they had been made aware. As nice as it was to not have to share the information with them myself, I was not thrilled about the spreading chatter.

I talked to them all before surgery and they all checked in after. Morgan and I had talked about trying to set something up with them when I was up for it. Little did I know that she had gone behind my back with my mother and set up a surprise. I was hanging out in my parent's room when Morgan came upstairs and said a package had just arrived but it was too heavy to carry up the stairs. curious as to what this package was, I walked downstairs and I saw the three of them all dressed up! I thought that they just came over for a visit until Morgan decided to tell me that we were all going out to dinner at my favorite restaurant. I hate being unprepared or being out of the loop. I like having a schedule in advance so I know what I have going on for the day, but it was fine. I had been crankier than usual and they were scared the whole thing would be a blown up mess. I don't know how they pulled this off. I honestly had no idea. Typically surprises don't work with me because I don't like them and because I always find out or guess, but they really got me this time. It was so nice to see them and catch up.

Though the news spreading bothered me initially, it was nice to know that I had genuine support from outside my everyday life. Opposed to other aspects of my life like dance and school, this support came from someone who I didn't have to see or hear from every day and somehow, I knew that the support was real and not motivated by other forces.

July 3, 2013

Around the time of the diagnosis, a friend of mine had told me to watch a movie called *50/50*. This is a movie about a man in a relationship when he is diagnosed with cancer. After witnessing a miniscule portion of her boyfriend's treatments, she leaves him. I had never heard about it so she told me the story and I wanted to see it. When I asked someone to watch it with me they said no because he knew about it and claimed that would never happen. I knew I wanted to watch it, but I just didn't have time. A little while after surgery when more of the walls around me started to cave in, one of my friends who would be heading off to college soon asked me to watch it with her in light of the recent events. I have got to say, it is one of the best movies I have ever seen. Regardless of the dark topic, it is so easy to relate to and it means so much more now than it would've prior to everything happening.

July 6, 2013

Nearly a month after the procedure, my steri strips are falling off and I don't know how I feel about that. I've always had this weird thing about my neck being touched and it just creeps me out. I also have a really bad gag reflux and can't wear anything on my neck. Being all stitched, taped, and bandaged, my neck issues were getting to be too much. Over time, I just accepted the bandages and everything because they weren't my top priority so my neck fetish faded, for a little while at least. Once everything started falling off, I started getting creeped out and sick about it. I was always the one who didn't care about scars or bruises and everything of that nature, but this really got to me. I couldn't even look at it. It was too gory, never mind how much of a reminder it was. I kept it covered so I didn't have to look at it because it made me so upset. I wouldn't even look in the mirror because that was the first thing I was drawn to.

Slowly I got to exit the walls of my house for short periods of time. The incisions weren't ready for sunblock, but they also couldn't be uncovered in the sun. Incisions burn much easier than skin and they would burn and never peel and fade. That was the last thing I wanted; I was already struggling with the light pink scar, no need for it to be bright red.

I knew I was going to be cooped up for most of the summer, but I did have a couple of fun things planned. I was supposed to set out to a student council camp, but once the dates for the RAI treatment were determined, those plans crumbled.. It seemed as though everything I was going to do that summer all washed away piece by piece as time went on.

Proceeding with some of the activities I had planned would only set me further back on the path to recovery and I was already more behind than I'd like and I didn't need to increase that difference.

July 8, 2013

Mid way through July, the process for the Radioactive Iodine treatment began. I stopped taking my Thyroid medication. Based on lab work, we were already aware my TSH levels were not where they should be, but because I chose to do the treatment so soon after surgery, there was no time to increase my dose before I came off of the meds. I knew the treatment would be difficult and cause my body a lot of discomfort, but I had not a clue what I was in for.

In an effort to make the best of my summer, whatever time that I might have had, I did as much as possible. Lacking a functioning thyroid, let alone a thyroid altogether, it was a challenge to stay awake for more than four to six hours at a time. I would take numerous trips to Panera to hang out with Ariana. She always made me feel better. Not a day went by where we didn't communicate.

It was summer, everyone was out living the life; going to the beach, going on vacation, hanging out with friends, and so on, and here I was caught up in an evil mess of medical junk.

At one point in the middle of July, I was so fed up with sitting on my butt and doing almost nothing, that I cleaned nearly the entire house. For the first time since surgery, I felt good. I was able to lift heavy items and move them and I wasn't in a lot of pain. It was the first time I felt like I was a normal human again. I had felt worthless for seven weeks just sitting there and watching my family take care of everything and wait on me and foot. This same day, I cracked my neck for the first time since moments before entering the operating room. I was hoping for an atomic boom, instead, I only got a single crack. Over the next couple of days I continued to clean and rearrange the house. I was quickly killing my body. At one point or another, the body builds up a tolerance for the physical pain and then **the pain of feeling worthless outweighs the physical pain.**

Shortly after I decided to call it quits on my excessive cleaning extravaganza, I headed to bed. I had barely fallen asleep when I was awoken by excruciating pains. I had shooting pains through my incisions and my legs and feet were spazzing uncontrollably. I didn't know what to do but I didn't want to wake my parents or concern them. I took some ibuprofen and fought through it. The pain and spasms subsided around 3:30 a.m. And I was able to fall back to sleep. I was concerned that this was another episode like the one in the hospital. I was sick and tired of being a burden on my parents. I wasn't a toddler anymore and I should have been able to take care of myself. I was moving backwards rather than forward.

July 17, 2013

When I was diagnosed, my pediatrician had told my mom to keep me away from reading things on the Internet. Obviously I didn't listen, but that's beside the point. She recommended a book written by a women who went through thyroid cancer. I got halfway through it before surgery but I was learning more about the operation and everything before I underwent my operation and it was scaring me. I put the book aside and I decided I would pick it up again after.

After my horrifying night, I decided to read some more of this book. I didn't want to go downstairs because I knew my mother would be upset with me. I stayed in bed and read. I got so caught up in what I was reading that I lost track of time. My mom came upstairs around eleven, concerned. I never sleep that late and she didn't know what was going on. She figured out what happened that night and after scolding me for being stubborn she let me finish the five pages I had left of my book before she made me go down and eat. I closed the book realizing that it was one of the best, if not the best book I had ever read.

July 24, 2013

The last week of July started the next step of the Radioactive Iodine Treatment; the no iodine diet. I knew it would suck, but I didn't think it would be too bad. I am a very picky eater and my diet consists mainly of fruits and vegetables, which I was allowed to eat on the diet so I figured I would be all good. My endocrinologist had given me a cookbook with a lot of recipes. I went through and marked out the ones that sounded decent, but I was banking on fruits and veggies for the whole two weeks. The first day of the diet wasn't too bad but as each day progressed so did the distaste for the food. I absolutely love salad and thank god I could have salad, but without dressing, it wasn't the same. Everything was so plain and disgusting.

July 26-28, 2013

Just after starting the diet, I was going to the Cape to play in a big field hockey tournament. It was the end of July and temperatures were in the high 90's off of the turf, never mind on the turf. On top of not being able to eat anything, I couldn't even drink regular water. The only thing I could drink was distiller water. I had the heat, the lack of thyroid hormone, lack of food intake, and just about everything else working against me. Being away from home and being on this extremely restricted diet was far too challenging for my liking. I couldn't get food from restaurants and I couldn't drink anything they had so I just sat there and watched everyone else. But the fourth day, I was sick of everything. I practically just stopped eating because it wasn't worth it anymore.

After the tournament was over, hell week began. This week had it in for me. Four trips into Boston in a matter of five days and too many doctors to count.

July 29- August 1, 2013

Monday started with lab work after a two hour hike into Boston at the crack of dawn. Tuesday was my day "off". Wednesday was a follow up with my surgeon and the first round of the iodine. Thursday I had a nice and long full body scan in the most contorted and uncomfortable position. Without a doubt, Friday would be one of the worst days of my life. Every part of swallowing the Radioactive Iodine had stressed me out since the day it was confirmed I would need this treatment. To go from being the person who won't even take an over the counter medication to being the patient fighting a disease that requires you to encounter the wrath of hazardous materials...unexplainable. I was a walking bomb, despite the fact that I wasn't walking and I wasn't in any space remotely close to human life for days.

August 2-3, 2013

On Friday morning I awoke sick to my stomach and more miserable than I had ever been in my life. I had to report to the lab to take yet another pregnancy test. As if that wasn't bad enough in my eyes, I had to then head up to nuclear medicine where I would become a human bomb.

We were running early and we sat around in Nuclear Medicine waiting for the results of the test to come back. I could've saved everyone a lot of time if they just listened to me. I took the prescription I was given for nausea and waited for the ever predictable results. The feeling leading up to the treatment was unexplainable. As each day passed and everything became more surreal, I found myself more upset about what had been put on my plate.

Once the pregnancy test results came back negative (should've just listened to me), I was taken into a room for the final steps. The iodine was ordered in liquid form as the pills are massive and I did not have any intention of swallowing pills the size of my fingers. The tech walks in the room and explains that my dose is actually two capsules. She was unaware of the liquid order and I was unaware I was so lucky to be given such a large dose. Shall I say DOUBLE WHAMMY? Not only did something get screwed up and I now had to swallow a pill at least and inch and a half long, but I was so lucky that I had to take TWO. Based on the scan, an extremely large dose of the iodine was needed to hopefully take action against these aggressive cells inside of my body.

After having a good 15 minute meltdown in the room when the doctors said that I had no other option but to take the pills, the first pill was exposed. It took a couple of minutes to take the first and then a couple of minutes in between, but I took them both and I will never swallow anything like it again. I feel that the fear of knowing I could not throw them up or choke on them made the idea of swallowing these horse pills worse than the fact that I had absolutely no desire to have this treatment.

To this day, every time I think back to that horrendous experience and I think about swallowing the pills and just everything about it, I grow sick. That is one thing I will truly never forget. That emotional scar may even be worse than the external scar from the surgery.

I was kept for observation for a short period of time and then I had to brave the two hour drive home and brace myself to be shut off from the world. The idea of vomit makes me cringe let alone the idea that the iodine can make you sick. I felt ok for the rest of the day and I was just really tired so I slept for most of the day. Early that morning I awoke so sick. I kept telling myself that it was just my head and I wasn't actually going to vomit. I held off for a little while and then that was the end. From that point on I was done. Everything about the iodine made me a biohazard and everything I touched became contaminated. In the weeks leading up to the iodine I had nearly stopped eating and drinking all together, but the first time I got sick was the final straw. I had been looking forward to the day I could eat food again and drink something other than distilled water, but none of that mattered anymore. I was so far gone into the "sick" world that nothing had any meaning. I continued to get sick for the next couple of days. The small breaks I would get from nausea lasted no more than five minutes and I would go back to feeling sick again. It was impossible to sleep or do anything else. I sat on my bed staring into the ceiling in between my constant trips to the bathroom. I don't remember ever feeling sicker. I just felt like crying but I knew that wouldn't make the situation any better. To top it all off, I couldn't be around anyone so my family just sat there helpless. There was nothing that could be done to ease my discomfort. My scar went from feeling bad to worse. All of the movement made the pain worse. I felt like the large incision was going to split open. Despite knowing that it wouldn't split open, the thought still existed. Some things are nothing but unpredictable.

A couple of days later I would be freed to the world of adults but not children. On this same day, I would be allowed to drink and eat like a normal human being. Now usually this day would have been great, but due to the circumstances, I couldn't even think about food.

I got up that morning and took a long shower praying I would make it through without vomiting, but I was denied that wish. I didn't feel well health wise, but I felt absolutely disgusting on the outside. Everything I touched felt dirty. I threw everything in the laundry. My pillows, blankets, and almost everything else in my room even if I hadn't touched it. All of my trash needed to be disposed of differently so I had a separate trash can in my room for all of that. I wore latex gloves for much of the process because I didn't want to be touching too many things that would then be contaminated.

After cleaning up a bit I felt a little bit better. My mother forced me to eat a piece of toast because I hadn't eaten in days and she told me that the only way I would start feeling better was for me to eat and drink. She was force feeding a sixteen year old. My stubborn side had once again kicked in, if it had even left. Needless to say, the radioactive iodine took a big hit on my body even before the after effects kicked in.

There's no telling what the long term effects of the treatment will be. To this point, I still do not have a strong sense of taste. What I lack in taste I certainly make up for in smell. I smell absolutely everything. It's the worst. I can sit here and worry about what the long term effects will, be which believe me, I've done, but it won't do me any good. As with anything else, only time will tell.

Once I was allowed out of quarantine, it was time to head back into the hospital for another lengthy scan. Once again I was put into a distorted and uncomfortable position and there wasn't anything I could do to change that. This scan was surprisingly shorter than the other one. I still was not feeling well and I was definitely feel the effects of the treatment. I had started to eat better despite not being able to taste the food I was eating.

Early August 2013

Within days of the treatment, I was more than fed up with my laziness. Regardless of what any doctor or adult told me, I was going to do something. I decided to go for a run. One mile. That's all I wanted was one lonely mile. A single mile has never felt so painful before. I felt like I was going to vomit, like my neck was going to burst open from pressure, and like my body was just going to collapse right there on the sidewalk. I had never been in worse shape before. I was mortified with myself. I was completely frustrated by my limitations and I will never accept any excuses for this poor shape, simply because there aren't any. There has got to be something that I could've done to remain in shape even if it wasn't long runs or vigorous training. Field hockey tryouts were only weeks away and I was back at square one. No matter how hard I trained, all of the hard work I put in was a waste. Nothing I could do would bring me back to the level I was at. My level of fitness was embarrassing. I cannot believe I let it get to this point.

I did my best to work my way back through all of the pain and distractions. Field hockey was my outlet and I was so frustrated with it that my outlet was gone. I knew no matter what, I was heading into tryouts blind.

August 11, 2013

After spending time with my father all day, I returned home. My sister and my mother were sitting in the family room. My mother asked me if I got her email and I had not. I checked my email and the strangest thing happened. It was an email from my endocrinologist with information about *The Fault in our Stars* by John Green. I had not yet read the book but I had heard about it. She gave me the general plot line and informed us that it would be being made into a movie. The novel is inspired by a patient of my endocrinologist, whose parents reached out to Jessica Smith to find people to be extras in the movie. They were only casting people who have cancer or who have had cancer. With my case being very similar to the main characters, metastatic Papillary Carcinoma of the Thyroid, Dr. Smith felt that this would be an awesome opportunity for me. I was unsure of my decision on this so I purchased the book. I got lost in the book and read it almost in its entirety in one night.

August 15, 2013

Summer was coming to an end and to be totally honest, I hadn't really done anything other than things related to my health. I took my first beach trip just days before tryouts. It was time to just sit back and relax. There was no sitting back and relaxing in the schedule as I had a load of Advanced Placement work to get done before school started. When the AP assignment isn't handed out until the end of July, it cannot be expected that the students can have it done in a month's time. AP assignments should and for the most part are, assigned before the end of the year. With everything I had going on over the summer, I didn't have time to spare. I hate last minute plans and having to rush to get everything done and I certainly do not procrastinate when it comes to schoolwork. Needless to say, I was thoroughly irritated by this assignment and its time management. Because of this predicament, I sat there on my one rest day of the summer, on the beach doing schoolwork. Don't get me wrong, it was great to be on the beach and having a sense of summer, but it should not have been that way. Once I got home from the beach, I was off to a student council meeting.

I managed to squeeze one more beach trip in the day before tryout as my final hoorah of summer. Between the STUCO lock-in, seventh grade orientation, Counter Attack field hockey clinic, summer assignments, and just the emotional roller coaster of everything going on, I was already overwhelmed, and the school year had not even started.

August 22, 2013

On the morning of tryouts, I awoke more nervous than I had been both my freshman and sophomore years. You would think that the anxiety would decrease as you got older and gained more experience, but something about this year just gave me a bad feeling. I knew my parents would be sitting on the edge of their seats at work praying there wouldn't be a phone call with any form of bad news. It didn't even come down to a JV/Varsity thing, but more of an individual performance factor. I came into the program as a freshman. I didn't expect to make varsity, but I gave it all I had. Looking back now, things were so different. I was granted the opportunity to work with a phenomenal coach. I didn't know her before tryouts, but I had heard a lot about her. Getting to work with her my freshman year was a blessing. She taught me so much about the game as I was still a beginner and I had never played outdoors before. Heading into sophomore year, I looked for individual improvement. I wanted to better myself from the previous year. I got involved with a club team and played throughout the entire offseason. I was even a member of the team that was named Regional Club Champions and attended National Club Championships where we faced some jaw dropping talent. At Nationals, we earned the thirteenth spot rank in the country. I hoped that all of my hard work would pay off. Sophomore year was a little less intimidating as I had been a member of the school for a year and I knew everyone. I was given so many opportunities by my coach and she made me the player I am. She always had faith in me, even when I didn't. The 2012 Hopedale Varsity Field Hockey team had an unexplainable bond. Everything just made sense. We had an incredible season that ended in the District Semifinals against a very competitive team that we came up short. We lost one to zero, an all too familiar feeling. Just a year before we faced the same team and lost by the same deficit. Not an easy thing to swallow. Coming off of the loss, I headed into club team mode. I had big plans for myself for the upcoming year. Off season went pretty well and I could tell my play was improving. I had reached a point where I was content with my play, but that didn't mean I would settle, I was always striving for improvement. In the midst of all of the offseason madness, which included a coaching change, I was diagnosed. At that point, and even now, the future is unknown. I didn't know what was going to happen and where all of the chips would fall. I knew either way I would miss some valuable time. I squeezed as many tournaments and practices as I could and I spent the rest of my free time out in my yard playing around. As with everyone else, my club team and club coach found out. They were so supportive and always reaching out to lend a hand. I've never been part of an organization so caring and supportive on and off the field. In the fall we would play each other and there were never any hard feelings.

I played up until the night before surgery and then it was over. I hoped that nothing would strip me of my love for the game. I couldn't wait for the day I could play again and hear my stick hit a ball for the first time; it was like waiting for Christmas morning.

I tried to make up as much ground as I could after surgery once I realized how much I had regressed. There was no time to play catch up, it just wasn't feasible. September 1st was approaching rapidly and I was in need of some good news. September 1st of my junior year was one that I was eagerly awaiting. College coaches would then be allowed to talk to individuals they wished to recruit. Unfortunately, due to the shortened off season, I hadn't been able to attend many tournaments so I wasn't expecting much.

There was no doubt that field hockey 2013 would be vastly different from the rest. Prior to the health crisis, we had been informed that the varsity coach would not be returning in the fall. My heart shattered when I read the email. She was one of the greatest things to ever happen to me and I would never be able to thank her enough. I had my suspicions of who the new coach would be. If I was accurate in my guessing, I would be excited. The 2012 JV coach was the daughter of a teacher I had had the pleasure of having for five years and she had been a substitute teacher for me on multiple occasions. Coincidentally, she got a job in Hopedale the year we transferred. I didn't think it was possible when I saw her on the first day of school. She taught seventh grade so I wouldn't have her as a teacher. Then she coached JV my sophomore year and I was so happy for her. With the coaching spot for varsity vacant, I figured she would take it. She's an incredible athlete and I knew she would do a great job. Overall, fall 2013 would prove to be an interesting season with the loss of five incredible starting seniors, a new coach, and my still healing body.

Junior tryouts were quite the experience. I thought that maybe I'd be able to pull my act together and everything would be fine. Man was I wrong. I played absolutely terribly and I don't even know what I was doing. I felt like I was on another planet. Day one session one was just the beginning. We had the preliminary tests. First off was the distance run. I had managed to squeeze a couple in before the day of tryouts, but all things went downhill that day. More than half done with the run, my incision was making popping noises and my collarbone was cracking. I was forced to stop running and call my mother. I knew that she was dreading this and the chances were that she was sitting at home more nervous than I was. I wasn't in panic mode yet, but I was getting there. I was in a great deal of pain but I was more frustrated because I didn't feel like there should have been any residual and lingering effects of the operation. I let it go and decided to suck it up and just play no matter what happened. I was playing like I had never picked up a stick before. It was a complete embarrassment. I can't even describe the experience more because it was so horrifying. Just as I thought it couldn't get any worse, the next session was worse than the first. After tryouts were over, I went home and reflected on how horrible my day was and what I could do to make it better. There was no way to turn around what had transpired, but rather to just move on and get my act together.

The final day of tryouts was slightly better than the rest. Things had calmed down a bit and I was playing with a little improvement, and I mean little in the lightest terms. Teams were made later that afternoon and nerves set in again. It was my third year, why was I in panic mode? I felt my heart beating incredibly fast as I walked down the hall and into the room where my season would be determined. Even after the conference with both coaches, I was still shaking. I couldn't pinpoint what was going on.

From the start of tryouts until the end of the season which could be the end of October, or the end of November, an athlete's life is devoted to the team, and to their academics of course. I knew that very rarely would I be lucky enough to find time to breathe let alone watch TV or sleep. Nothing more than a sacrifice all athletes make, but it's because we love what we play.

Once tryouts were over and the practices had begun, summer was REALLY over. I never looked forward to it, but this year I was even more upset over this yearly event.

August 26, 2013

My feelings about the first day of school this year were drastically different from those of others. Summer 2013 had set new records for me. I've always been busy and active during summer and had a blast doing the things I love and being with the people I love, but this summer just wasn't right. I can't say it was horrible in the sense that I am so thankful to be where I am and have some of the journey behind me, and I'm ever so blessed to have the support that I do, but this summer sucked. I went through things I never imagined. I don't think anyone thinks it'll ever be them getting the news that they have cancer or other horrible things, I know I sure didn't. I've always walked away from summer feeling accomplished and happy with the memories I made, but the memories made over this summer were the kinds of things you wish you could just forget about. I'm not saying I want to forget about everything that happened this summer, but I wish I could put it out of my mind and remember when I want to.

Aside from the feelings of resentment towards the summer from hell, I hadn't left my mother's side for more than a couple hours at a time since the day before surgery. I was skeptical as to how well I would do away from her if it was any other year, let alone this year. On top of attending school for just over six hours, I had practice after and I would not make it home until around 6 p.m.

I always said that I didn't care what my scar would look like. Looks don't mean much to me. I always get so annoyed with people who spend excessive amounts of money and who spend all this time perfecting themselves. If that's what you feel like doing, then by all means go ahead and do that, but it doesn't make you any more of a human being than anyone else. I don't care about bruises and bumps from sports or anything like that. I mean in 8th grade I walked around with a black eye for almost 15 weeks. If you play sports or do any type of physical activity, or you're just plain old clumsy, the bumps and bruises and other types of injuries shouldn't come as a surprise to you. You can't possibly think that in playing a sport your body will remain untainted, guaranteed you will get hit with a ball or tripped at some point; that doesn't mean you need to make a big deal about it. it's all in the name of the game. When I was asked how I felt about a big scar plastered across my neck and asked if I wanted a plastic surgeon to stitch me up after surgery, I said no. It wasn't necessary for all of these extraordinary measures to be taken over something so little and virtually meaningless. Nothing could change the way I felt about this until my operation was over. I wasn't phased by this new feeling until my steri strips started to fall off. I kind of just went with the flow until I started to have trouble looking in the mirror. When the first layer of bandages started to fall off, I refused to look simply because it creeped me out, but at the time it had nothing to do with my feelings towards the scar. Slowly as everything else began to fall off, I had an even harder time looking in the mirror. I knew with each day I would heal more and in no time, you'd hardly even know I had two scars on my neck. But as summer moved on, I was not impressed with my healing. Maybe I thought it would be instantaneous and it would only take a couple of weeks. By the end of the summer I had only looked at my neck in the mirror maybe a handful of times. Within the first two months following the surgery, I used multiple bottles of scar remover gel and my mother even purchased silicone gel bandages to assist in the removal. It wasn't going away or even fading. I wore t-shirts every day and I even planned on wearing t-shirts every day to school. I couldn't bear to look at it myself, never mind being in a building with more than five hundred other students and staff members staring at my neck. I was not ready to answer questions to everyone nor was I ready to have all eyes on the "sick one". I tried to keep the situation as much on the down low as possible and I intended to keep, but the wounds are daily reminders of what I went through and all that I am.

Even six months later, I can't look at the scar with ease. The minor incision looks great and there is little residual scarring, but the large incision is hard to look at. The first thing I feel every morning is the pain in my incision from laying down and the first thing my eyes look at when I go to get ready every morning. There is no way to avoid the wrath of the incision for even the slightest bit of time. It's there from the second I awake until the last second before I slip out for the night. There's no way around it, and that's that.

August 27, 2013

The night before the first day of school, I headed off to bed early. Those plans backfired and I found myself going to sleep much later than I had anticipated. My mind was just wandering off and I was in panic mode. It took me hours to fall asleep and even then I was in and out of sleep. Needless to say, it was not ideal heading into the first day of school with a scrimmage after.

When I awoke in the morning I was very nervous and hesitant. I didn't have any other options other than to suck it up and go to school anyways. The way things would turn out that day were unpredictable.

It seemed like the day dragged on forever. Each class felt like it was three hours long when really they were all under an hour. It was tough not having my mom either. I had had an extended summer which also didn't make things easy.

The only thing that got me through the day was knowing I had a game after school. Once the bell rang and sixth period was over, I was free until the scrimmage was over and homework began. With a huge rebuilding year ahead, I was nervous going into the scrimmage. I didn't know what to expect. The only thing I knew was that there is almost nothing I hate more than losing. Losing was not an option. Standing on the turf waiting for that whistle to blow was like waiting for pigs to fly. It took forever and once that whistle blew, the ball was in play and the result would be determined by the desire to win. Both teams wanted the win and it was anybody's game. The first goal was scored pretty early into the game and the goal was for us. At that point, most of the nerves had faded and the real game had begun. My team settled down and no one was in panic mode. We came out with the win, but that was no indication as to how we would play for the rest of the season. This scrimmage was against one of the weakest teams we would play all season and we had no idea what we were in for.

The second I walked in the door, it was time for the homework meltdown to begin. It was only day one and I had hours and hours of homework. There was a lot of paperwork and loose ends here and there that I needed to take care of on top of the piles of homework. I sat there and moaned the entire time. It was only the first day and I was in over my head. I knew junior year was going to be a struggle, but I didn't have a clue as to what I was in for. 179 days to go! My body was not ready for all of this. I was in desperate need of a break and there wasn't any break in sight.

The next couple of days dragged on and field hockey was the only thing that got me through the day. I was still nowhere near happy with my play and it seemed like it was getting worse. Nothing was going my way and I was so done and the year had just begun.

The day before the long weekend was the ever so dreaded picture day. Could not have cared less what I looked like. Once I got called down, I walked into the auditorium. I thought the auditorium was supposed to be a happy and welcoming place, but something about the auditorium at Hopedale High didn't make it so welcoming. I got in line and got my name sticker and waited for my turn. The guys who do our pictures have a track record for being rude and touchy, but nothing prepared me for what was to come. I get in position and the photographers looks into the lens and asks me to remove my necklace "because it's creating a glare." Well, I've got news for you, I wasn't wearing a necklace... or anything else on my neck for that matter. I was really offended by this. I don't expect people to just automatically understand or know what happened, but I never saw this coming. I was in absolute awe, took the picture, and walked away horrified. I forgot to tell my mom after practice, but when the thought crossed my mind again, I told her and she was really upset. I found out later that she had told my dad and he was even more upset. It's only a school picture, I don't understand why the company is so hands on and touchy. The whole situation just makes zero sense and it probably won't ever make sense, but what's said is said, can't pretend I didn't hear it. You would think that adults would be more mindful and mature about the situation and not open their mouths so quickly, but it's possible that I have had more adults say things than kids.

September 2013

The beginning of the school year was rough. I sat there and hoped each day would get easier, but it never did. The season progressed and we were doing ok. Unfortunately, certain factors were challenging our progression. There were a few members of the team that were talking trash about some other members of the team and they were really making the targets feel bad. For some reason, I happened to be one of the targets of the talkers. These people think that we aren't going to find out about what they're saying and get upset about it. It's a given that not everyone can like everyone else, but in the wise words of Coach, "We are a family until November. Learn to get along with one another." The incidents had been reported to coach and she had addressed the situation with the entire team. I thought things would get better, but they didn't. The same people continued to talk and because we had had multiple meetings and nothing was being resolved, the athletic director was brought into the "final" meeting. Between Coach and the AD, they knew who the talkers were and one more strike and suspensions were going to be handed out. The inability for us to work together as a team was apparent both on and off the field. We had just lost one of the biggest games of the season at the peak of the drama. The team was easily beatable, but without teamwork, each player is out on the field as an individual playing for herself. The game was an absolute disaster and a devastating loss. I went home after the game in utter disbelief of what had just transpired. It took me days to move on from that game. Constant replays of what happened and what I could've done better so the end results were different. Moving on from that game was a challenge, but the only way to move on with the season, was to move past that game and for the team to get back on track. The team quickly got back on track and we were playing like we knew we were capable of. It doesn't necessarily take a win to be playing really well, it is more so about playing as a team and playing the absolute best you can.

As the season continued on towards tournament time, we were the team to beat. We were dominating our games. Here and there we would have our issues, but as soon as we saw them, we made attempts to fix them. We came up with some big wins, one of which gave us the Dual Valley Conference title. Beating the team we had previously lost a very close game to, our biggest rivals, was the highlight of the regular season. To me, it was the first game we played 110 % together as a team. We beat them to every ball and just dominated play and it was huge. At this point, the season wasn't over, we still had a couple of tough games to play.

Our "pink game" was coming up. Hopedale Field Hockey dedicates one of the final home games of the season to breast cancer. We all wear pink in support and we raise money to be donated to a research foundation. The field hockey team chose an online donation fund through Longstreth and we donated our raised money to both thyroid and breast cancer.

Our pink game fell against a very tough opponent this year. A very talented team that would surely put up a good fight. It would be a battle to the last second.

Due to the slow healing of my incision, it was determined that I would wear protection on my neck when playing. It wouldn't be surprising if I got hit in the neck by a stick or a ball so it was better to be safe than sorry and protect the fresh wound. I did well in the beginning of the season being consistent with taping it, but then my gag reflex started kicking in and I could no longer tape it and not have any issues. I switched to a different type of tape which was working much better. I liked this tape better because it blended with my skin better and it was less noticeable...or so I thought. During our Thyroid/Breast cancer game, one of the players on the other team looked at me and asked me what was on my neck. Before I could even respond, if I was actually going to anyways, she peeled it off my neck and said, "I'd appreciate it if you wouldn't wear that." I was shocked. Who has the indecency to do something like that in the middle of a game, never mind the fact that it was a fundraiser for cancer? I don't expect people to see the tape on my neck and know that it's a thyroidectomy scar or that I'm battling cancer, but I also never in a million years imagined that this would happen. I thought she would apologize after seeing the scar on my neck that she made visible, but she never did. I guess I gave her a little too much credit. For some reason, this really upset me. How did having tape on my neck affect her or how she played? I still can't figure it out. I'm not one to talk on the field, especially in response to an act of such poor sportsmanship. So many things came to mind and quite frankly, what I really want to do was snap at her, but I knew it wasn't the right thing to do. Since that game, I really struggle with taping my neck because maybe it does affect people in some strange way that I just don't see. Most days, I don't tape it. In the back of my head I know I shouldn't care because I'm doing what I need to do in order to continue playing and avoid an injury, but it bothered me so I just take it day by day. I hesitated with telling people about what happened because maybe I was responsible. After the game a couple people asked where my tape had gone and I just responded that I didn't know. Little did I know that another member of our team saw it happen. Slowly people started to figure it out. I wasn't too good at hiding my anger either so it quickly became evident to my coach that I was upset to say the least. For a while I refused to tell her, but when I asked her if I could go talk to my mother, she forced me to talk to her first. I tried to refrain from telling her, but she knew me too well and she knew how to get the answers she wanted. Before long she pieced together the reasons behind my discontent and she was not happy to say the least. When I told my parents, they were upset. My mother was curious as to what happened to my tape. I went from having tape on my neck to not having tape on my neck and she didn't know what happened to it. It wasn't like I got taken off the field and had the opportunity to take it off and put it in the trash. I tried not to make a big deal about it and I never disclosed which girl it was on their team because I wasn't positive. A very dedicated man to Hopedale sports takes pictures at almost all home games for each sport. He happened to be there and when he gave us the pictures, I tried to figure out which girl it was because I knew what her stick looked like, I just wasn't sure what number she was. Regardless of their terrible sportsmanship on the field, our team pulled out the win and that's all that mattered in the end. As long as we maintained our composure and didn't slip to their poor level, we were golden. Hopedale Athletics prides itself on our sportsmanship, and that shouldn't change based on what teams are on the other side of the field. That day, we played for all the people that can't because they're not as lucky. We raised money for a great cause and we left it all out on the field.

With less than a handful of games left, each game was tournament preparation. Each and every game needed to be played like it was our last. There was no room for any breakdowns or injuries.

We faced a tough loss to an undefeated team at the very end of our season. We played great in the opening half, we just couldn't capitalize on our opportunities and in the second half, we just didn't play our game and that allowed them to come out on top. Heads up, we walked off the field. Although we were disappointed, we were proud of how we hung with the big names. Hopedale was going to be a force to be reckoned with in the tournament.

- -

SEASON REFLECTION

Regardless of where we end up going and what titles we win or lose, I'm proud of the accomplishments we made over the course of the season. Not much was expected of us considering the rebuilding year we had ahead of us, but even with a hard schedule for the season, we did enough to earn one of the top seeds in CMASS DII. But on an individual level, I was not at all pleased. I walked off the field almost every game knowing that I could've done more. I thought this season would be my best yet, but to be honest, it may have been my worst fall season. I am my own worst enemy and I refuse to give myself credit. The team this season also suffered. You put 20 + teenage girls together and put them up against each other for playing time, things are bound to get ugly. Unfortunately a handful took things too far and ended up really hurting other people. With a new coach on board, I feel some people felt they could get away with more. Athletes who I adored last year really showed their true colors this season and I lost respect for them. The word TEAM was lost at points throughout the season and that hurt us. Where I would typically use field hockey as my outlet for bad days, doctors' appointments that don't go the way I would like, and just stress relief, I found myself at a loss. Field hockey lost that magic because a couple of people made it a chore, opposed to something I look forward to. Eventually, all of the things people say will grow to be healed wounds, but you can't repair the damage you caused. You can't make up for lost time, and you certainly can't change the friendships you broke. There are the players that can prevail no matter what people say, but there are also the perfectionists who take everything that's said and remember it every time they're playing the sport. No one's necessarily to blame for this, but I wish things didn't get to this point. Too many people were hurt and the fun was taken out. And it's not just other teammates who have an influence, the parents on the other sideline have as much of an impact as the other athletes. When other parents who know so much about the sport are questioning the playing time, or lack thereof, for certain players, it reassures that you're not being biased. I watched a little piece of my sister be taken away each day. Standing there knowing there was nothing I could do to make it better was even harder. Her confidence was completely taken away and it's questionable if she'll ever gain it back. I think that if it weren't for the thousands of dollars we had invested into the National Field Hockey Festival at the end of November, she would hang up her stick and never pick it up again. She has so much passion for the game and she was always so happy to be playing. She's had her fair share of bumps along the road and field hockey meant the world to her. To watch her go from being so happy and in love to almost hating the sport, words can't describe the feeling. Different things that were said by both parents and other athletes confirmed that things weren't the way they were expected to be.

All things must come to an end. Every team gets knocked out at one point whether they get knocked out champions or knocked out losers, every team's season ends. Our season came to an end with a great deal of tension. As I walked off the field for the final time this fall in my Hopedale jersey, I was full of regrets. I wish I didn't let the parents get to me. I wish I didn't let my teammates get to me. I wish I wasn't so critical of myself. I wish I didn't play so poorly all season... All of the "I wish", but there was nothing I could do to change that. The season was over and all of those regrets would hang over my head forever. It would have been much easier to lose if I didn't have such an awful season. I never worked my way back to my play pre surgery. I don't know why or how, but I think that sucked the life out of me. I could sit here for days on end questioning myself, but it won't do me any good because I don't have any answers.

The season serves as a learning experience for all of us. We learned things about ourselves, our teammates, and the importance of working as a single unit. Although it sucked having to learn it this way, only good things could come from it.

The regrets of the season got more obvious each day. Once I moved on from the initial shock of the season being over, as happy as I was that I didn't have to put up with the bullshit anymore, I wanted to travel back and redo the entire season. I went to the Semifinals games to watch.

Nothing was more painful than not being in my jersey with my team playing for a bid to the District championship game. It was nearly 30 degrees outside and I was sitting there every second wishing I was playing.

I had high hopes going into this season on a personal level, but mediocre expectations on the team level. I let myself down with the goals I had set for myself and that's something I'll never be able to fix. On the team side, we had a pretty good run. Our record was better than I anticipated, based on the rebuilding year we had, but it could've been much better had the aspect of "team" been there. When all is said and done, the season had its ups and its downs and all we can hope for is to do better next year. We get so close every year, one year we'll get there. No one can say we didn't go down fighting and that's what I'll take out of this season. It was a learning experience for all of us. Individually, I took out of the season that every turn you make in life will bring someone new trying to tear you down. It's what you do in spite of these people that make you a better person striving for excellence.

November 2, 2013

Following the conclusion of the season, the results of my blood work came back quite surprising. The results showed that I am registering an awful thyroid hormone level in my body. I can't tell you why or how that's the case, but the labs have spoken. I'd been feeling pretty crappy and extra tired, but I figured it was just in response to the stress of junior year and the nerves with field hockey. Maybe that has something to do with it, but my TSH levels, or lack of, are more likely the reason for that. My dose was increased and my next labs are to be done at Children's Hospital. I thought I was going to be able to escape that place until June 2014, but doesn't look like that's going to happen.

November 5, 2013

With the fall season being over, it was time to focus on Festival and college. I knew I wanted to play in college and I had been talking to a couple schools but I had my eyes set on five or six schools I was really interested in. I had the opportunity to meet one of the coaches for my top choice the day after our season ended...probably not the best time, but I really liked her and I loved the school. I knew I couldn't hang up my stick for three weeks so a couple of the girls from the varsity team and I decided to go down to our field and run a practice. Nothing big or extravagant, but we weren't ready to give it all up. Trust me, we all could've used the extra time to be doing homework and everything else, but the sport meant too much and the season ended too soon. After three months, our bodies were programmed robots to change and go to practice after school, then to go home and do homework until the early hours of the morning and then sleep, get up, get ready for school, and repeat. If I didn't do anything I'd probably just go home, lay around, eat, and then start my homework at 10 o'clock that night. Instead why not pretend the season isn't over and do what we love until we can't do it anymore?

After a deeply depressing meeting where we had to hand in our uniforms not to play again until the end of August, we headed down to the field to pretend we were still in season. Just running back and forth on the field dribbling and working on skills I was too scared to try during the season, I felt free. I was free from parents and teammates who weren't in the same place and whistle-happy refs. Just fooling around and taking shots on an empty net I felt like I was given a new set of wings and I remembered why I loved the sport so much. Of course, today was the day my stick work and speed and play that I was missing all season decided to make its appearance. I don't know why, but just my luck. No matter how hard I tried all season, it was lost in space, and the second it doesn't matter, it comes. Maybe it was the pressure or that I was trying too hard, but whatever the reason, despite the fact I was thrilled that it was back, couldn't have been worse timing.

We continued to go to the field to keep our stick work up and just simply to have a good time. I would be heading to Florida in three weeks to play in a huge tournament that could determine my future in the sport, it was not time to choke. I still find myself bored out of my mind not having a dedicated practice time every day despite the fact that I *have* hours and hours of work to do, it's just not the things I want to replace that gap with.

DANCE

Once the season ended, the urgency on making a decision about dance intensified.. I don't go a day without thinking about it, but I can't bring myself to make that final decision. I can't do everything I would like to, there's just not enough time or money, but I try to do as much as I can. Often times I bite off way more than I can chew and I dig myself a hole. I know this decision needs to be made in the best interest of myself, but I do take into account other people. My parents support me in absolutely everything I do, but dance has put them through a lot. It's extremely time consuming and quite frankly, a chore. Jealous parents make for awful teammates. In saying that, I also can't let the parents and students sway me one way or the other. If I were to make this decision process easy, I would go back because I love it and I worked so hard for all of my skills and everything I have, but it's just not that easy. I don't want my mother to have to go through the drama like she has in the past. I have one friend at the studio my own age and then there are a few younger kids that I love to death. Aside from the politics and other shenanigans, my health needs to be brought into account. First of all, I don't know if my body can handle it. I'm already up to my eyeballs in stress and lack of sleep, what would adding another activity do. I just don't know if my body could tolerate it, and to be honest I'm terrified to see what limitations my body has. Prior to surgery, the only thing that stopped me from excelling was my fear and even then I was still progressing and moving forward. I doubt that's the case now. Finding out may just make me more resentful. Second, how would I be treated at this point? I know that whatever decision I make, I'm letting someone down; all of the younger kids that looked up to me as a role model, my teachers, my best friend who has been there suffering through the struggles by herself, my parents, myself... It's easily the hardest decision I've ever had to make. I've thought so hard and long about this and I always find myself unable to pick a side. How can I just give up something I've worked so hard for? Am I supposed to just forget about it and give it all up? It seems impossible and time is ticking.

I promised myself I wouldn't let any part of my health dictate any activity and I would never miss something because of it. Well I've broken that promise like a thousand times. I've missed out on quite a bit because of doctors' appointments and because I can't keep myself awake long enough to do anything other than school, field hockey, and homework. I'm also allowing my health to play a key role in my decision on dance. All things I said I'd never do.

- -

HOW CANCER CHANGED MY PERSPECTIVE ON LIFE

Each day I wake up thinking it's all a nightmare and none of this ever happened. You can watch all these people you know or have heard of, get diagnosed. You can see and listen to all of these foundations and just overall, all of the drama surrounding the idea of cancer, but one thing's for sure, you NEVER think it's going to be you. I knew more than a dozen people who have had cancer, have cancer, or died from cancer, and their stories truly touched my life, but even growing up so close to the disease, I never ever, once thought that I would be diagnosed with cancer. My heart breaks every time I see someone or hear of someone who has cancer show up on their door step. I'm not sure that anyone sees it coming, but I didn't have a single symptom or anything. All of this came about at a yearly physical. And even then, it was thought to be nothing. I've had a few big surprises in my lifetime, but this is by far the biggest. I've had much of my life planned out for a couple of years now. I know things don't always go as planned, but I like to have a general idea of what the schedule looks like in advance. Last minute plans and changes don't go over well with me. I didn't have cancer in my schedule, never mind a surgery, RAI treatment, and everything else that came with the package. I'm not a flexible person so being told the surgery needed to be performed soon didn't sit too well. I didn't have time, let alone the desire for the process. I wouldn't even acknowledge that this was reality. I figured as time passed I would slowly learn to accept everything that would happen, but time doesn't make any part of this easier. Time after time, I find myself wishing for my old life back.

- -

*THE TRUTH ABOUT SUPPORT

To sum it all up...be careful who you trust! There is no better support than your family. Going through this as a teenager was probably more difficult than if I had been out of high school, but going through it at any point sucks. Unfortunately, high school is just hell and adding something like this too it doesn't make it any easier. Now, in saying this, I'm not saying I didn't receive any support from friends, nor did I want or expect to, but everyone jumps at the bit to tweet, text you, or reach out to you in any way, and then when you need the most support, no one is there. People feel that if they're friends with the "sick" girl, then they look like great people and they'll get all this attention, but in reality, they're just making themselves look ridiculous. Do you think that we don't notice that you're only acting friendly because you're trying to get all of this attention? Being sick doesn't make you stupid, just vulnerable. A cancer diagnosis doesn't just affect you, it affects your entire family and all of the people around you. You may be the one who's sick, but everyone else has to sit there and watch you suffer, knowing there isn't anything they can do to alleviate your suffering. Sometimes sitting there helpless is worse than the suffering. I watched my sister go through two surgeries and the last one was rough. There wasn't anything we could do and she could hardly communicate with us. **When push comes to shove, the people you can fall back on will always be your family.**

It's always interesting to see how things turn out when everything is done. People you would never expect anything from are the ones who turn out to be the most supportive. I didn't want anyone to see me after surgery and I didn't want the attention. I did my best to keep it a secret from the second I was made aware of the diagnosis. I told less than a handful of people about the biopsy and I knew they wouldn't tell anyone else. I knew from the beginning that the situation would get blown up and I'd be surrounded by fake and two faced "friends". As soon as the first post was made, I was screwed. My hope at keeping this quiet was lost.

In dealing with something like this whether it be you or someone close to you, you learn what truly matters. Life's not a walk in the park and it's not about anything other than being the best that YOU can be and not worrying what other people say. What you choose to do with your life is your choice, but you are the one who has to deal with your choices. For my entire life, I've sat here and worried what other people think of me and I've let that stress me out. Who cares about it. You'll meet thousands of people in your life and not everyone is going to like you. Trying to change yourself so people will like you won't get you anywhere; you can't please everyone, it's just not possible and you'll waste a whole bunch of time trying.

In battling through any difficult time, not just a disease, no one truly understands how you feel and what you're going through. People will speculate and make their assumptions, but you're the only one who knows how you're feeling. For me, I chose to keep my treatment plan and as much of the other pieces of the journey to a limited number of people. Most people thought I would have surgery and everything would be all done, I liked it that way. It made it easier to avoid the fake attention. Unfortunately, that wasn't the case. I will forever be reminded of the memories, let alone the scars and the medicine and the blood work, and the doctors' appointments. The disease is a lifelong sentence of paranoia and life lessons. In some cases, scars, medicine, disabilities, a life in the hospital; the list goes on forever. Someone who is diagnosed will never forget hearing the words "you have cancer." You hold your breath every time you have a doctor's appointment praying the disease doesn't come back and that you'll get good news. The journey never ends, it's always a part of your life whether you choose to accept it or not.

I look at finding who truly matters in my life one of the biggest lessons. You always hear that high school is where you find out who your real friends are, but cancer gave that line a whole new meaning. I *really* found out who my real friends are. Like I said before, there will always be the people who are not fans of yours, that's life. But in the face of a tragedy, while some people swim, others sink. Everyone tweets, posts, texts, and says they'll be there for you, but it's all a lie. It's certainly not easy to deal with people who are constantly sick, in and out of the hospital, and people who are time bombs, but what if it were you. Would you want people there for you if you were in their position? I know cancer brought out the worst in me and I'm thankful every day that my family puts up with me. The people I never expected to be my support ended up being the best I could have asked for and ironically the people who I thought would be great, turned out to be the worst. I don't resent these people, but I certainly don't waste my time and energy on them. People are going to make up rumors and try and tear you down, no matter how low you already are, but that's their problem. You want to go and make others' lives miserable to make yourself feel better, you go for it, but just remember you will be the only one who has to deal with the consequences. I'll sit here and take it for now, but one day, I'll catch a break and karma will hit you like a grenade when you least expect it and that day will be the day when everything will make sense.

FLASHBACK~
AMERICAN DREAM PROJECT~
MARCH 28, 2013

Towards the end of freshman year, one of my dance teachers asked me if I had ever thought about auditioning for Cirque Du Soleil. At the time, I had never even considered it. I had been to countless shows and I loved the idea of going somewhere in acrobatic industry after high school. At the same time, I was falling more in love with field hockey and I was now looking into playing in college. As I became more interested in field hockey and more involved in school and club field hockey, I began to resent dance because it got in the way of so many other things I wanted to do. I never liked to show anyone outside of dance what I could do because I don't like putting myself out there. Most people didn't understand why I spent so much time at *dance*. Hardly anyone knew what I could do and I liked it that way. After a pasta dinner at my house, people saw pictures and they began to beg me to do these "cool tricks." They began to talk about it and before I knew it, almost everyone knew it. Randomly, a couple people would ask me if I was in Cirque Du Soleil or something like that. When I would say no, they would tell me I should audition. Until then, I had never thought about it, but now I questioned whether I should look into it or not. I started doing research and I talked to my teachers about it. It seemed pretty crazy and I was scared of rejection. It took me a long time before I decided that I would try. With the help of my studio and a friend, I began putting a video together. Once I began on this journey, dance didn't seem so miserable. I was in the studio everyday working for something bigger than an activity to fill space until graduation. The project was kept on the down low and very few people were aware. With all the bitter dance moms and their kids, I didn't need any more drama. Shortly after submitting my video to their talent scouts, I got an email back from them. I was terrified to open it and see what may come of this, so I didn't open it for a couple of weeks. I never wanted to give up field hockey, and I wanted to have a normal college experience, but this seemed like something I could do after graduating from college. I don't have any confidence in any of the activities I participate in and I'm NEVER satisfied with my performance in anything. Acro was the one thing I allowed myself to admit that I was better than mediocre at. Still, there's always something I could've done better. I received the email in December and I didn't open it until February. Unfortunately, I was not 18, and therefore, I could not begin my journey with Cirque at the time. I took this as a matter of age, not talent. Maybe I'm good enough, just not old enough. Looking at this predicament optimistically, I continued to strive for this goal every day in the gym. This became my American Dream. At the same time as all of this was going on, we were reading *The Great Gatsby* in English. The novel was all about the impossibility of the American Dream. As an assignment for this reading, we had to put together a poster about our American Dream and what it meant to us. It only seemed right for me to do my dream of being a cast member of Cirque du Soleil. I was hesitant to share this with anyone in fear of it getting out, but I chose to do it anyways. Coincidentally, as I was putting the project together, I was going through the beginnings of what was much more than anyone ever anticipated. With the due date of March 28th, I had already undergone the initial feeling of an enlarged thyroid, blood work, and an ultrasound, and still, I did this project with not a clue of what would happen once the biopsy was done. The project turned out much more successful than I thought and has even more meaning now than it did when it was handed in. The projects were handed back just days after I was diagnosed. Still struggling with the diagnosis and everything else that was going on, I chose to not look at it. I find the timing of this project and the way it coincided with my diagnosis to be ironic.

When I was diagnosed, it came as a complete shock. Even through all of the testing I never once thought it would be what it was. My first thought was all of the time I would have to take off. I cared more about that than the logistics of what was happening. It didn't occur to me right away everything that could be put on hold or completely taken out of my life. My dream of being in Cirque Du Soleil was something that needed to be put on the back burner.

Maybe the disease was the world's way of telling me to slow down and relax.

This dream cost me. Everyone thinks acrobatics is all cool and easy, but it did some pretty bad damage. I was one of the primary lifters at the studio. Lifting people who ranged from peanuts, to people who were taller than me. All of the lifting put a lot of stress on my back. Some days were worse than others but the pain was always the worst at the worst possible time. Every time it would start to get better, I'd do something stupid and it would get worse. I tried multiple things in hopes of getting better, but nothing seemed to work. I kept saying I'd take a break and let it heal, but there just wasn't a good time to do that. Once I was informed I would need surgery, I figured that would be my time to heal so until then, I would just have to push through. Just a couple of days before my surgery, my back reached its breaking point. It was the final event for dance of the season and I couldn't have been happier. I ran a road race that morning and my body had had enough. It was time for a break. I struggled to make it through the two recitals that afternoon, but I had no idea what the next day was going to bring. The last recital of the weekend brought some big gifts. I knew that that could have been my last time ever performing. The performance team recitals are always a little crazy and unorganized. Due to some mishaps, the order of dances was rearranged. I ended up with a couple of dances on top of each other. Two of which were intense acrobatic pieces. Still dealing with discomfort from the previous day, I did the minimal during warm ups. After fighting through the tears on stage during one acro number, I had three minutes to change and go on again. I had ice packs down my costumes and parents and teachers helping me get dressed. I was doubtful I would make it through the next three pieces, but I had no choice. The numbers were so close for two people that we were changing backstage with anyone who was there. As I was walking on stage for the next piece, barely holding myself together, I was pulling an ice pack out of my costume and throwing it off stage. This one being my hardest acro routine, the chances of me making it through were slim to none. For the last 5 or more years, my mother did not need to help me change and get ready in between pieces because there was enough time and I was capable of doing it myself. Because of the lack of time, she came to help me. I've never been so rushed and discombobulated in my life, never mind the fact that I could hardly walk I was in so much pain, let alone lift 115lb people. With one more number to go, things were getting progressively worse. I was told I did not need to go on for the last piece, but in the back of my head, I knew it could be my last time on stage dancing, and the choreographer of the piece would probably be upset if I did not perform. I sucked it up and went on. All of the hours, pain, stress, and politics of the sport made me question my choices, however, my dreams of being part of Cirque made the negatives worth the persistent struggle. From day to day I learned more about myself through the sport as I traveled through the peaks and pits of what being a competitive dancer brought. Just after this project was due, I found myself deep in thought over what affect cancer would have on this aspect of my life.

November 25-30, 2013

Looking forward to such an event made things a little easier. I would soon be in the nice weather, do what I love, while escaping from the negatives of life at home. Despite not being a fan of traveling, I was excited to go on a mini-not so vacation. Once we landed in West Palm Beach, FL, I knew I was going to have a great time. I would love to go to school down in FL, but I would get so distracted that I wouldn't be able to get my work done.

Although it seemed like it was a vacation, there was a lot on the line. The tournament was filled with thousands of girls all competing to be looked at by college coaches. Almost every girl there wants to pursue a collegiate career in field hockey. Playing on a field with 21 other people at the same time, you have to stand out in a coach's eyes. The great part is, not every coach is looking for the same qualities in the players. While some may be looking for speed and determination, others may be looking at the skills of an athlete.

The pressure to be recruited is huge. Families pay thousands to go away for a couple of days to an event like this. My sister and I decided to sign up pretty late in the game, increasing the stress, and we booked our flights very late, adding more to the cost. The pressure was on.

Once returning home, you have to hope that you did everything you could and there was someone out there who appreciated what you brought to a team. It was only a matter of time until you would see if the trip was worth it.

Heading home was bittersweet. I am so grateful to have had this opportunity, but it meant returning to the not so swell life: going back to school, the cold, and most importantly, the drama associated with high school.

December 2013

With the final weeks of the year approaching, it was important to make them count. Winter break was on its way and I just had to push through a little while longer before I had some time to myself. The end of the year was pretty quiet. I hadn't had any doctors' appointments for a while. Track was as dramatic as ever. After the pressure to do Winter Track was laid on, I decided I would, not because I wanted to, but because I felt I needed to. Every day I regretted my decision, but my hands were tied and I felt that I had done everything I could to improve the situation. I contemplated quitting almost every day. Being miserable for three hours a day was three hours I didn't have to immerse myself in the countless hours of homework I had. I found myself crankier than ever, but as a captain, I owed it to my team to stick it out and finish the season. In the past Spring Track has been far more enjoyable so I hope things get better. Losing some of my best friend as they moved on to college definitely contributed to the tense atmosphere of the track team. Fortunately, a couple of friends made the misery and tension more bearable. Getting ready to commit to college for field hockey while preparing for the National Indoor Qualifier added fuel to the fire. I would pick field hockey over track any day. Needless to say, sports took up most of my time. With that being said, sports are also largely responsible for my ability to make it through the day.

December 21, 2013

Right before Christmas break, I was lucky enough to go to the Beyoncé concert with my best friend. Now, that stuff isn't really my thing, but I love Beyoncé so I decided to go. It was truly one of the best nights of my life and I'm thrilled I went. The beginning was a little rocky, but in the end totally worth it. While the opening act was on, the vibrations were radiating through my neck, making me feel like I was on a different planet. I had never experienced this feeling before and was scared I was going to have to leave. It seemed like the act went on forever. Eventually, when it ended, I had a little while to recover and let my neck relax. Fortunately, with Beyoncé's performances, I wasn't as bothered by the vibrations. Had there not been this hollow cavity in my neck, I would not have felt this. For me, this was one more reminder that I can't escape my past or the experiences I have acquired.

We were fortunate enough to have third row seats right by the stage. Being that close to such a star made everything worth it. It was a Friday night in Boston and the sights were pretty frightening. All of the college kids were out on break living it up in the city, absolutely wasted. When the concert was over around 11:30, we had to trek a mile to meet our ride. The single mile walk felt like 10. It was pretty cold and the people in the city were scary. Holding onto each other we sprinted through the city to find our ride. Seeing everyone too drunk to function is exactly why I will not be like that in college. We watched people nearly get hit by cars because they were fooling around and not paying attention to the lights. After not getting home until 2 A.M. I was really questioning why I was leaving for a field hockey tournament three hours later. Overall, I'm thrilled I went and I couldn't have enjoyed myself more!

December 23, 2013

The end of the year was tough. On top of everything going on, it was my favorite time of the year. As much as I hated the cold and the weather, I love the holidays. Something about this year felt different. The year had been one big roller coaster and I was just waiting until I got to the bottom to jump off. Things were busy as ever and there was little time to do Christmas shopping. When my parents asked me what I wanted, to myself I responded to be cancer free, but to my parents I said to be set free from Children's Hospital. There is honestly nothing more depressing than being in that building. You can fill it with the greatest people alive, the best toys, or anything else for that matter, and it will always be bad news for someone. One day when you're getting good news, someone else is getting terrible news. I'm so grateful for everyone who I have crossed paths with in Children's: my surgeon and his team, endocrinology, nuclear medicine, phlebotomy... But it would be so thrilling to have never had to spend so much time there.

Two days before Christmas it was time to head back into Boston for some labs. Nothing said "welcome to winter break" more than a trip to my least favorite place. I thought that some good news would be a Christmas miracle, but really it was just a miracle to be able to spend time with my family and be as healthy as I was, even if I wasn't cancer-free.

When we got to the hospital, the renovations in the lobby were complete. We were gone long enough for them to finish renovations! Sadly, yes, that is exciting.

Once my tests were done, it was time to do some last minute Christmas shopping with my mother. We patiently waited for the phone to go off with the results of the labs, but it wasn't coming quick enough. We figured it wasn't too important so we would probably find out after the holidays.

Six weeks prior, I had the same labs done and I was registering zero thyroid hormone. Still unsure what that means, but my dose was increased and labs needed to be repeated. This time, when the results came in, only a very slight increase in levels. My treatment was changed and the dose, once again increased.

I knew that once the new year hit, my follow up scans and ultrasounds to check the intended success of the surgery and the RAI treatment would be scheduled. I haven't and won't be able to rest easy until I know I'm cancer free and all of the torture was worth it.

Before I knew it, my favorite day of the year had arrived! No gifts are needed that day. The greatest gift was being with my family with everyone happy and healthy.

Winter "break" was flying by. It seemed as though everyday was something and there was no time to relax.

THE DANGERS OF
THE INTERNET

I've found it really easy to get myself caught up in everything. The worst thing I could do, I've done more than once. I knew when I did it the first time I shouldn't have, but there is something that compels me to continue to do it. Research. From day one I was told not to ever open a web page on the disease. I knew it would just overwhelm me, yet I still chose to do it. I should've learned the first time when I watched videos of biopsies and read all about people's personal experiences to the point that I freaked myself out over a practically painless procedure that at the time had no influence on my life. When my pediatrician told my mother the diagnosis, she also said to not read the Internet and offered some book suggestions. My mother told me, and too late, already had opened and read multiple stories, which certainly didn't make me feel any better. Almost every night when my homework was done, I would do a little research. Around the time of surgery I refrained from opening the Internet because I was already freaked out way more than I needed to be.

After surgery, I purchased a couple of textbooks and novels. I wanted to know as much as I could about the disease.

For a while, I was too busy and too preoccupied to continue reading... probably a good thing.

Late in December, I fought myself caught up in the habit again, only this time, instead of freaking myself out, I just grew extremely angry. I found a website where people had posted pictures of their healing scars at different points. By six months, most people's scars were virtually invisible. Mine remains raised, bright pink, and very painful. I was beyond frustrated. I'm half the age of most of them, I'm supposed to heal quicker.

Time after time, people I hadn't seen for a while would say, "you look so good. I wouldn't even know you're sick," but the first thing I notice it the thick, pink line going across my neck.

January 2014

To open the year up, vacation was extended when a storm hit and dropped a foot of snow and freezing temperatures. These two days were a blessing. I was smart and I had all my work finished and I was ready for school, but I just wasn't mentally prepared to go back. With junior year, even when all your homework is done, there is still an endless list of things that need to get done, I'm just always way too exhausted to start tackling that list. There's always something to be working on or something to be organizing or cleaning. Two more days were two more days. The day before heading back after 16 days off was the National Indoor Qualifier for club field hockey. This tournament would determine whether or not we made it to Nationals in March. I went in with little hopes of pulling out of our bracket never mind qualifying. It was a nail biter but we managed to pull out and qualify. It was a long day out at Mt. Holyoke but totally worth it.

This win meant that a trip to Virginia and some more college recruiting was in order. Unfortunately this trip falls the weekend after returning home from Costa Rica. The opportunity was too good to pass up though so I went ahead and booked flights.

The National Indoor Tournament would be huge for college recruiting and it was critical to be in perfect condition to play.

Late January 2014

The weeks leading up to February seemed to pass with increasing stress. Each day, the things that needed to get done kept piling up. I hadn't been feeling well since December but I never really thought anything of it. Track was exhausting and school was too stressful to put into words. I couldn't wait for the season to be over. February would be a very busy month that included two trips and a busy month of junior year. On top of that, I continued to get sicker. After ignoring my mother's advice to skip a track meet when I was at my worst, I nearly passed out in the middle of my race from pain. I had shooting pains through my heart and lungs and I was beyond dizzy. At that point, I knew she was right and I should've listened. The second I got home from the meet, I went to the doctor. I was told that I had some pretty intense infection and told to stay out of school for a couple of days and not return to track for a month due to the fact that I had decreased breath sounds and low oxygen levels. Unfortunately, quite a few rumors had been circulating and I owed it to myself to make people aware they were false. It was championship season and there was no time to sit out. I took the 5 days off and competed that weekend. I was nowhere near my personal bests and really struggling to make it through an eight second race. Once I seemed to start to get better, I just got worse again. Just days before leaving for Costa Rica, I felt the worst I had felt since the RAI treatment. I could hardly breathe and the pains in my chest and lungs were unbearable. My mother felt it would be smart to go back seeing as I'd be flying to a different country without her in a couple of days. The doctors said there was fluid in my lungs and it wasn't getting any better. They put me on a couple of prescriptions and told me to contact them immediately if anything should happen.

The track season ended and a huge weight had been lifted off my shoulders. I was sick the entire season and absolutely miserable. I would be out of the country in just two days, only problem being I had yet to pack.

Time was ticking and I wasn't in any way prepared to leave. I was extremely apprehensive as I had been sick for the last 8 weeks.

Fortunately the season ended and I was blessed with a school cancellation the day before I left. This would give me ample time to pack and get my act together, but of course I was not productive and ended up saving everything for last minute. When I finally did pack, it was a project and a half. I always struggle with over packing, but it was really bad this time. Packing for a different climate and making sure I have everything if something were to go wrong was nearly impossible. I made an attempt at crossing things off of my list of things to do, however, I failed miserably and ended up staying awake really late.

COSTA RICA

With the International Club at Hopedale, I had the opportunity to travel to Costa Rica during our February Vacation. Though I was not sold on the idea when my mother signed me up, I am forever grateful. Despite this trip having nothing directly to do with cancer, indirectly, it did. This trip has had more of an impact on me than almost everything else I have done in my life.

February 14-21, 2014 (Costa Rica)

When I finally did go to sleep, all I could think about was my mixed emotions about the trip. I woke up and finished the final touches on packing and headed off to school. We were leaving two hours after school started so we all had our luggage and not a soul was focused. Fortunately, our parents could come and say goodbye to us prior to departure. For some reason, it was really hard to say goodbye. We took a bus to the airport and got through security and to our gate. We had quite a bit of time so the fun began. We flew from Boston to Miami and that flight was smooth. From Miami, we had quite a bit of time before taking off for San Jose. Once we left Miami, we would no longer have Wi-Fi or cellular service until we got to the hotel. We boarded our flight to San Jose and sure enough, we had a major delay. We were sitting in the plane for two hours before the issue was fixed and we were ready for takeoff. We were set to arrive in San Jose around 10:25 P.M. But with the delays and everything, were going to be much later than that. Once we landed, we still had to go through customs which takes quite a bit of time. We were finally on the bus and on our way to the hotel. We were introduced to our tour guide and given a little bit of information that everyone was too exhausted to comprehend. Thanks to one of our chaperones, the tour guide decided to give us an extra hour to sleep as we arrived much later than anticipated. The rooms for that night got a little scrambled but we were leaving in 5 hours anyways so it wasn't a big deal. Everyone looked dead the next morning. Traveling had taken everything out of us and we had been in school all week leading up to the trip. Surprisingly, everyone pushed through and no one complained. We got on the bus and headed straight up the mountains to the community we would be in for the next four days.

When I pictured what Costa Rica would be like, my image was very different. I had an image of all beaches and beautiful waterfalls, and a week of luxury. I figured the community service part would be quick and painless. Much surprise, it was nothing like what I had imagined. It was really late when we landed so it was difficult to get an accurate image of San Jose. When we were on the bus on the way to the hotel, I was sitting with Megan and we thought we saw mountains off in the distance but we were both in denial. The next day, while on our way up the mountains, our suspicions were confirmed.

With some minor complications just prior to our arrival in San Pedro, the community we would be working in, we were slightly delayed and forced to switch to smaller 15 passenger vans to complete our trip.

We picked up our tour guide about an hour and a half into our two hour trek out of the city and into the mountains. He hopped on the big bus and was all peppy and I could tell I wasn't going to like him. We were all exhausted and cranky and here he was like he had just had 12 cups of coffee. I looked at Megan, Morgan, and Alexa and said, "It's gonna be a long four days..." When we finally got to the community center, I was in utter shock. It was a very poor community, almost vacant. It looked like a scene right out of a movie made hundreds of years ago. We were welcomed by member of the community and we got an introduction to our community service projects and what the general itinerary for our trip would be. I had mixed emotions about everything, but I did my best to keep an open mind.

After our introduction, we visited a major coffee processing plant. I have never seen so much coffee in my life, much less what it actually looked like. We took a tour of the plant and learned about the lengthy process.

So much more respect for coffee now! After spending a couple of hours in the plant, we got to go to the restaurant side of the place and try the coffee. I will never be able to drink coffee the same way again. The process is mesmerizing and the length of time it takes, and never mind the fact that their coffee is 100 times better than any coffee I've ever had. Before we left, we all had to buy coffee for our parents because it was so good!

After leaving the coffee plant, we headed to the hotel we would be at for the next four nights. We were still in a very poor and vacant looking area full of mountains and things I had never expected.

It was a pretty quick drive. The geography was astounding. There were no guardrails and if you weren't paying attention, you'd be off the road and on your way to death. The road were 90% dirt and the only pavement present was on larger highway type roads.

When we arrived at the hotel, it was quite a culture shock. I saw one cabin type building and then some smaller cabins. I was unsure if they belonged to the hotel or not. I knew that we were staying at an Eco lodge, but this was much more "Eco" than I expected. The main building didn't seem big enough for 30 people, but it was possible that that was where we were all staying.

Our tour guide began to run off names of roommates and it was concluded that the smaller cabins were where we would be staying. The teachers would be in the main building. My roommates and I for some reason were not assigned to a cabin but that was eventually fixed. There were two larger rooms with two levels, two small single cabins, and three small cabins attached to each other. My cabin was the last one on the group of three. The boys were lucky and got a what was massive in comparison to ours, room with a big bathroom and three bedrooms and a kitchen. The senior girls also got a big mansion. Now *mansion* there is not was it seems. It's nothing like our homes now, but in the situation and under the circumstances, they were mansions. We all headed up to our cabins were in awe when we opened the door. Not necessarily our cup of tea, but I knew we were in for an experience.

While some struggled with the lack of television and other material goods, some of us just struggled with the nature aspect. I couldn't have cared less about a television, but I'm not a big fan of bugs and the wilderness.

Once we settled in, we showered and got ready for dinner. We were told there was hot water and that we were the first ones to stay. Taking the first shower was quite the shock, it was probably 40 degree water. Absolutely frigid. I've never taken such a quick shower and been so cold before in my life, not even in the dead of winter in Massachusetts.

Dinner was, well... Interesting. I'm a very picky eater to begin with, but this was more than I could handle. I could not believe what was on my plate. Later on, we all decided to call it "mystery meat" because it truly was a mystery. The food all together is another story. A food night was put on a couple of months before we left so we would have an idea of what to expect. That was just a little taste of what was to come. I figured I'd be all set, I practically went two full weeks without eating in preparation for treatment, what was a week of no food. I did not have the slightest clue of what we were actually getting. Some meals were much more familiar than others. I thought salad was a universal item so that would be my intake. Unfortunately, salad is not served very often in the smaller less touristy areas. Despite being nothing but creeped out about the food, we all managed to survive. Once we got to the tourist areas, the food appeared much more appealing.

After dinner, we went to the boys' room for a little bit before heading to bed.

The first night at the Eco lodge was a challenge. A couple years back I developed anxiety, nothing major, but enough to put me out on occasion and it's all because once I start thinking about something, I don't stop. For a while, the "attacks" seemed to disappear and I forgot about it. Oddly, the first night at the lodge I was presented with another. As I was falling asleep, I could not turn my brain off. I was thinking about all of the bugs and the "mystery meat" and I just got really nauseous. Once I fell asleep, I would be fine, but I could not find the off switch. I decided to try putting music on and hopefully that would put me asleep. Fortunately it did, but it took hours which meant that I only managed to sleep for two or three that night. That night made me want to get on a plane and go home right then, but that was not an option and I'm glad it wasn't.

When I woke a few hours later, I was fine and ready for the day. We had breakfast and got ready to head to San Pedro. When we got there, we all met on the soccer field and discussed what we hoped to learn and what our goals were. Once we finished that, we got started on the three projects. We were divided into three groups and sent to one of the projects.

My group started with painting. We had to sand the walls and the prepare to paint. The walls were white and blue to begin with so I figured that's what we would paint them. Much to my surprise, we were given lime green and turquoise paint. I love that color combination so it was really exciting. We took a break for lunch and then went right back to work. It was Sunday which meant that there was soccer going on all day on the field. The field was located by all three projects so when we had our breaks we would all go over and watch them play soccer. After our day of work was completed, we got to play soccer with the children in the community. There were very few students on the trip who played soccer so it was quite interesting. The kids from Costa Rica were insanely good, and we couldn't even kick the ball. Everyone got sick of the soccer so we taught them some American games like capture the flag.

When it was time to leave, someone requested we stop and get coffee again because it was so good. We also needed to stop at the little store and get water and stuff. The coffee was just as good as it was the day before. We picked up our groceries and headed back to the Eco lodge. Back at the Eco lodge we cut up our pineapple. One thing that had stood out to us was how good the pineapple was. We joked about getting a pineapple, but thought it would be frowned upon. Once we were told it was ok, we bought one. Everyone looked at us funny when we were cutting it up, but it was totally worth it. The pineapple was quite the production and drew quite a bit of attention.

On the way back to the Eco lodge that night, Jonathan was driving our van. He left Morgan, Alexa, and myself in charge of the music. With quite the selection, we landed on one with a slightly inappropriate name. Curious, we decided to play that one. The second the song began to play, Jonathan ordered for us to change it. That song soon became one of the memories we will never forget. Once dinner was over later that night, we would continue this and listen to the song in the lodge.

Dinner was in an hour so we all got to take showers and get ready. That night might be one of the most memorable nights of the trip.

We all were talking about how we wanted to go zip lining and one of the chaperones asked Jonathan if we were going to have that opportunity.

It wasn't scheduled in our itinerary, but the option was being explored. One of Jonathan's many tricks was that he worked for an Adventure Park in Providencia in the Cloud Forest. He decided to offer us the opportunity to go to the Park for a discounted rate. The only issue with this was that we would have to leave San Pedro before lunch and have lunch in the vans because the car ride was two hours straight up a mountain and no joke, into the clouds. Not a single person did not want to go so it was official, we would be heading up into the clouds to a wild Adventure Park.

When we first got to our cabins and were exploring, we opened our curtain to find one of our friends in the top floor of his cabin in the wide open window attempting to twerk. Morgan even captured it on camera before he noticed us. From that moment on, a joke was made about me teaching him how to twerk. On top of the joke with him, he asked our tour guide if he knew what twerking was and if he would want to learn how. It was never really a question, we were going to teach him anyways.

The chaperones all knew about the picture of him attempting to twerk so they went along with it and told me I needed to teach him how. It's no secret that yes, I do know how to twerk, but it's also not a secret that I don't twerk for the general public.

Don't ask me why I did it because I don't have an answer other than caving in to peer pressure, but that night I was told I needed to teach Jonathan and Cam how to twerk. Apparently this drew a whole audience and each with a camera out. Jonathan told me that if he twerked I would have to learn a dance native to their country. I wasn't thrilled about it, but I was willing to do it so he would twerk.

He was interested to hear some of the music we listen to so we played some of the music we had on our phones. After listening to some, we begged him to play the "secret" song. Though terribly written and overly repetitive, it has to be the funniest song I have ever listened to and one of the most unexplanatory stories behind why I like the song.

After our music extravaganza, he agreed to twerk. Cam went before Jonathan because Jonathan still had no idea what twerking even was. For a while, everyone had left and went to their rooms, but most came back for this. After Cam went, I had to learn a Costa Rican dance before Jonathan would twerk. That was quite interesting. I had no idea what I was doing but for some reason could not stop laughing. Once that was finally over, Jonathan was ready to twerk. He immediately started laughing and chickened out, but it didn't end there because I knew he would eventually do it, and he did! The chaperones were all laughing so he suggested they learn how...again, this is all on video. I had to twerk with them, but two of them did make an attempt at twerking.

I don't have the slightest clue as to why this even happened or why I gave in, but despite the embarrassment and awkwardness, I will NEVER forget this night. With majority of the action on video, I watch it every once and a while and it's just as funny now as it was the night it happened. The "secret" song has now been downloaded and listened to repetitively and it one of the strongest jokes we have with Jonathan. We even convinced him that it was okay to play it in the car and that the chaperones wouldn't care. We only played it when there was our certain group of 10 with our two chaperones.

We didn't have the slightest clue what time it was but when someone realized, it was time for Jonathan to go home and for us to retreat to our cabins. However, my roommates and I didn't go to our room, we went to the boys' cabin. Though it was only the second night there and it was already really late, it was a tradition to go to their room every night. The laughs didn't end when Jonathan left or when we left the boys' room. The laughs ended around one in the morning when we found a cockroach in our room. Everywhere we turned, there was some type of bug flying in the cracks of the ceiling or crawling out from the walls. The issue became that neither me nor my roommates wanted to remove these bugs from our room. After at least 20 minutes of debate Morgan stepped up and took care of the mystery flying bug while I locked myself in the bathroom out of terror. The cockroach got away that night so we just made sure all of our bags were zipped tight and headed to bed.

The morning came quickly and it was a struggle to get up. The temperature probably dropped thirty degrees overnight and even with sweatpants, a sweatshirt, fuzzy socks, and hood up we would shiver constantly. I even brought a blanket with me because I can't stand hotels. I was so creeped out by the bugs and everything that there was no way I would be sleeping under the covers. After the first night, I realized multiple bites on my back and legs and got even more creeped out. I started tucking in my pants to my socks in hopes of avoiding the bites. Once we were all ready, we headed down to breakfast which of course was an adventure.

After breakfast we headed to San Pedro to do DAY 2 of the community service. The second day was farming day for my group which meant hours in the organic coffee farms with Jonathan. We got started as soon as we got there. The coffee farm was a couple of minutes away from the community center so we rode in the back of the truck to the farm. It was quite the adventure seeing as though we were standing in the back of a pickup truck with the geography of the mountains. Surprisingly, we made it alive. I felt like this was the most laborious of the three tasks, but definitely the most entertaining. The only downfall to the farming was the infinite amount of bug bites we ended up with. Jonathan had come up with nicknames for the four of us...Morgan was MP, Megan was Broc, Alexa was Big Al, and I was #twerkteam. The setup of the coffee farm made sight challenging and we were all spread out through the farm, but using our nicknames, Jonathan made sure to know where we were. When we began fertilizing the plants, the five of us started throwing fertilizer at each and throwing the buckets. Fooling around made the time pass faster and we were still getting the work done more efficiently than anticipated… it was a win win situation. Once lunch time rolled around, we headed back to the community center. Before we could eat, we went to the school. Prior to leaving for the trip, we were told that we could bring school supplies to the children because they didn't all have sufficient supplies. Some generous companies gave us almost 50 backpacks to donate to the children. Each student on the trip was given two that we would be fortunate enough to hand to the children. The way the school hours work there are different than here so there are two sessions each day. We caught the morning session. They all came out of their classroom and stood in a semicircle and we were opposite them. Jonathan explained to them who we were and what we had for them. They got to come and pick one of us to take a backpack from. The little girl who came to me had been at the community center the day before and had earned herself the nickname, Diva. She was super cute and super sassy. One of our chaperones took a picture of the two of us and her new backpack. That is definitely one of my favorite pictures and experiences from the trip. I have never in my life seen children so happy to receive a simple backpack with a couple of supplies in them. It was the most adorable and heartwarming experiences. After they got their backpacks, they gave us a tour of their school and played basketball with us until it was time for them to leave and us to go have lunch.

As usual, lunch was a production. I felt like it was scene from a movie. It never failed to have some entertainment value to it. The food at the community center was much better than the food at the eco lodge. Once lunch was over, we were going to tour the Quetzal forest and hopefully see one. Although it sounds boring, the suspense made it exciting. From the second you entered the forest you needed to be silent or you would risk scaring away the bird. To get to the forest was very little uphill and a lot of downhill which only meant that the trek back up would be a straight up. On the way down, we were in a single file line all clenching to the ground to stay on our feet. Every few steps someone would manage to slip and sometimes even fall. It was hard not to start laughing, but if we laughed too loud we would ruin our chances of seeing the Quetzal. We got to the bottom of the hill and waited for the professional Quetzal Caller to see if he could find one of the birds. When he did, he came back and we all headed over to the location. He took our phones and took pictures through the microscope so we could have the image and be able to see the beauty of the bird. He was almost at the end of the line and the bird got spooked and flew away. Following the birds departure, we headed to the main lodge of the Quetzal Forest and we got to see hummingbirds and hang out. It may not have been the most interesting thing we did all week, but it had a relaxation factor to it that was definitely beneficial considering we were all absolutely exhausted by this point.

We headed back to the Eco Lodge for the night and continued on with the typical night routine: Shower, dinner, "cult" bonding, bugs, and finally bed. I decided rather than showering in Antarctica, I would go and steal the boys' shower. Without a doubt one of the best decisions I have ever made. I completely forgot what it was like to be able to breathe while taking a shower, never mind the fact that you could move from side to side in their bathroom whereas in ours, you could barely fit a single body in let alone move. After showering, we headed down for dinner where the food that night was not too bad. Unfortunately, the main component of our entertainment was missing that night. Jonathan could not stay for dinner that night so we began our "party" earlier. Party was in our room...Alexa had downloaded the first episode of Gossip Girl and she was determined to get us hooked. The boys decided to join us and just ignore the fact that Gossip Girl was being played. We turned the lights out, pulled out all of the snacks and candy we bought and covered up in blankets. The boys were bored out of their minds and kept making irrelevant remarks. Once the show was over, we turned the lights on to find one of the boys passed out in Megan's bed. We tried to wake him up, but we weren't having much success. When he finally came to, he asked where he was. It was relatively late, but one of the boys couldn't let the night end there. He had to dress up in women's clothing. Megan's dress was hanging over the ladder to the top bunk to avoid wrinkles so he chose to put the dress on. He was amused by the "high-low" style and turned the night into a show. He struggled to put the dress on and take it off, but that didn't stop him. He started cracking up, as did everyone else, to the point that we couldn't even speak we were laughing so hard. Once we were all embarrassed for him, he took the dress off. The boys headed back to their room and we got ready for bed. The chaperones had come to do room check as he was in the dress and they thought it was hysterical as well. Not even a minute after the boys left, the cockroach made its third appearance. This time, no one was prepared for it. I was on the bed so I had no idea what the "ummm GUYS," and we all looked down at the floor. I screamed and jumped up. I was standing on the bed and without even thinking about it, I attempted to leap over Megan's suitcase and out the door. Only problem being that I had fuzzy socks on and underestimated the length of the jump. My feet slipped out from underneath me and I face planted just inches away from the railing on the porch. My knees caught the brunt of the fall and I was screaming. The boys hadn't even made it back to their cabin, which mind you was only about 15 yards from ours. They starting laughing and came back. They asked what happened so I told them and one of them was kind enough to come back and kill it for us, FINALLY! My knees hurt so bad but I couldn't stop laughing. If only this was on video...I felt like it was a clip from America's Funniest Home Videos. Once we all collected ourselves and stopped laughing, we headed to bed, resting easier knowing that the cockroach was dead.

The next morning was no different... wake up to the freezing cold barely able to move. We all got ready in our typical order and headed to breakfast. Headed to the community was different on Tuesday. This was the last day we would be in the community and that was tough. I had anticipated looking forward to this day because it would mean the beach and settled areas were in the near future, but this was almost as hard as the day we arrived back home. Our day in the community was cut short so we could squeeze the Adventure Park into the packed schedule. The community had planned to do a lengthy formal goodbye, however time did not allow for that. On the final day, my group had the cementing project. The designated work had already been completed so we exceeded the expectations and moved forward with the project. Around noon time, we completed the community service and our time in the community had come to an end. We all met in the center and some prominent members had prepared speeches for us in a modified farewell celebration. Jonathan translated the speeches for us and the room was so silent you could hear a pin drop. In order to get fit everything into the schedule, we needed to eat lunch on the way to the Park. The community center had made a cake for us and thanked us for everything we did and said goodbye. They prepared our lunches and gave them to us as we walked out for the community center for the last time. Once we got into the van, of course with the "cult of 10 and Jonathan as our driver" we headed to the Adventure Park about two and a half hours away. When we got to a certain point we needed to switch to a van with four wheel drive. We missed out on the truck where we would sit outside of the cab so we were stuck in the 20 passenger van. This had to be the worst car ride I have ever taken. I thought the rest of our travels had been straight up and down mountains, but certainly not anymore. This ride was STRAIGHT up a mountain. One of the chaperones was struggling during this ride. She was having a panic attack and the other chaperones were all ready to be sick. The ride was relaxing aside from the slight chaos brought on by fear. The landscape was breathtaking and being in the clouds was so strange. When we finally got there in what felt like 10 hours later, everyone had crashed. I didn't know how much of the action I would take part in, but I knew that I would need to be daring because I would regret it later. Jonathan introduced us to the rest of the staff and they put us all in harnesses and explained the four events to us. We split up into three groups and my group headed to the Tarzan Swing first. After seeing the first person go, I doubted I would do it. A couple people in, the release malfunctioned and someone was stuck up in the tree in the harness scared to death. After that I was certain I would not go, but for some odd reason I decided that I would go ahead and go for it. I got strapped into the harness and hooked into the swing. I was pulled back and the countdown began. The second the line was pulled, I experienced the biggest stomach drop of my life. As scary as it was, I do not regret it at all. We rotated through the other stations. The next one was not scary at all. We climbed about 40 meters up the inside of a special tree and then repelled down to the bottom. The final station was sneaky. They put you on a zip line for about 10 meters and then when you get there they hook you up to a swing that has no additional harness and you have to jump off of the bridge. When it was my turn to go, people thought it would be funny for me to go upside down. Once I jumped off and got through one swing, it was safe to flip. I swung upside down in a straddle for the remainder. Easily the scariest thing I have ever done but again, totally worth it. The final station everyone went to at the same time. It was called the Monkey Bridge. There were 2 wires about 6 feet apart. You held onto one with your hands and walked on the other. Once everyone was finished we got in the vans and headed back for the night. We got the back of the truck this time. It was getting late and the temperatures were dropping but we were not going to let the opportunity to ride in the back of a truck through the clouds pass. It was about a 2 hour ride back to the Eco Lodge and definitely one of the best memories of the trip. There was a speaker in the back of the truck and Jonathan let us blast the music. No one would even be able to hear the music, we were thousands of feet in elevation and in the middle of the clouds. On our descent downwards, Jonathan would stop at certain points and show us some things. About halfway through the trip, if you looked off in the distance, you could see the lit up Pacific Coast where we would be heading the next morning. It was really dark and the only sources of light were the stars above. As sad as the day was, it is definitely one of the greatest parts of the trip.

The next morning we awoke to shivering yet again, however, it would be the last time we would be in this situation. As rough as the Eco Lodge was with the bugs and the wilderness, it's definitely an experience I am glad I had the opportunity. I think that everyone walked out of the lodge with a greater appreciation for what we have and the quality of our homes.

We *enjoyed* our last meal at the lodge before we departed on our exciting adventure. After saying goodbye, we got into the two vans and headed out. A short distance into the three hour trip to Manuel Antonio, we stopped and loaded into four trucks with seats in the back. Of course, our cult got the red truck with the speakers and Jonathan as the driver...well we thought that was a good idea. Our truck was the first to go so we didn't all get covered in the dirt like the three other trucks did. However, the journey took us through the mountains and all around down to the coastline. About half way through the tip, the motor started making a funny noise and we had to stop. We had no idea what was going on but it couldn't be good. We were scared we were going to have to split up and go in the other three trucks and that would have ruined the entire day. Eventually, the truck started again but we didn't know how long it would last. Shortly before we arrived, we stopped at a Pulparia in the middle of nowhere and got drinks. Once we took off we rode through rivers and got to the point where we would say goodbye to Jonathan. The big tour bus would now pick us up and we would be on our way. This may have been the hardest part of the trip. We had all grown so close to him and he made the trip so entertaining and memorable. Megan, Morgan, Alexa and I got one final picture with him and tears may have been present. We got on the bus and he ran through and said goodbye to everyone and we were on our way. Oddly, everyone was silent. At this point everyone was beyond exhausted but it was also a challenge to say goodbye. We headed to the Shana Hotel where we would unload our luggage and then head to lunch and the beach.

We got to the resort and we knew we were in the tourist areas. The hotel was gorgeous and far different from the Eco Lodge. We got our room keys and headed to check out our room. Opened the door and all jaws dropped. Everything was white and I had never seen anything so pretty before. The bathroom had about three different rooms inside of it and the porch had a chair set and a porch swing. We only had about 10 minutes for the four of us to get changed and ready to leave. After getting changed we headed to the restaurant and then to the beach. I've been fortunate to travel to some pretty nice places, but this by far was the most gorgeous thing I have ever seen. I wish I could live there for the rest of my life. I had never been in the Pacific Ocean so I could cross that off my bucket list. It was a good thing this part came after the community service and the lodge because I don't know if we would have survived if it went the other way. We all bought gifts and souvenirs for our families and ourselves so we could remember this trip forever. We watched the sunset on the beach and then headed back to the hotel to shower and get ready for dinner. The boys were all so happy to finally have food somewhat American. After returning to the hotel, we determined that the party was in our room and we were not sleeping all night. The night was so bittersweet. The next day was our last day before we were heading back to reality, which no one was ready for.

That night we watched some of the Olympics which we had missed most of, sadly. The lack of sleep continued to make others glazed over in exhaustion, but it didn't really affect us. We were all having the time of our lives and nothing would stop us. The final morning we got ready and headed for breakfast. We said our goodbyes to the beauty of the hotel and got on the bus. The day was overall boring but relaxing. We visited an oxcart place and then took pictures with the world's largest ox cart before getting lunch and getting on the bus for the hike back to San Jose. When we got to the hotel and got into our rooms, we had to get ready for the final night's dinner. There, we would get our superlatives and wrap up the trip and share a memory. Once again, party was in our room and the last night would be the best yet. After returning from dinner, everyone put on comfy clothes and came to our room. It was hours full of laughs and then Megan and I fell asleep for a little. When teachers came in for room check, they didn't even bother to send everyone to their rooms so the party lived on. I woke up around 12:30 am with my hair braided and suspicious silence. I fell back to sleep and so did Megan. Thirty minutes later, we were both awoken to one of the boys jumping on our bed because his favorite television show was on. The boys left around 2 am and we headed to bed shortly after. We needed to make sure we were all packed because the next day would prove to be the most dreaded day of the trip. Waking up was a struggle because everyone was upset that we were leaving. After driving to the airport, everyone became increasingly upset. Like always, getting through security and customs was a pain but after getting through everyone made some final purchases and got some lunch and it was time to board the plane. The flight from San Jose to Miami was relatively smooth but the flight from Miami to Boston was rough. We got off the first and ran through security and customs and barely made the flight. We thought that we would have enough time to get dinner but without that, we got on the plane less than 5 minutes prior to gates closing and that's with one chaperone yelling at the attendants. When we finally got on and ready for takeoff, they told us that we would not be taking off promptly due to mechanical issues. We rushed and panicked for nothing and almost no one had food and it was going to be at least five hours before we landed. We waited for takeoff and I had already managed to complete most of my homework so it was rather boring. Walking into Logan was so depressing. The trip was over and so was the greatest week of my life hands down. We were all heading back to reality and all of the things I needed to get done hit me the second I stepped off the plane. It was the wee hours of the morning when we finally arrived home, but mom and dad were not going to go to sleep until they found out more about the trip considering we had minimal contact for a week.

The first couple of weeks after returning home were very challenging. I missed everything about Costa Rica and I would have done anything to go back. I'd take everything that came with it, even if that meant the food. Seeing as everyone had the same mind set, the "Postarica Depression" became well known. After our two days of recovery, it was time to return to the nightmare. It was a struggle to go more than five minutes without drifting off in class. As expected, the theme question of the first couple days home was "How was Costa Rica?" which we all found so challenging to put into words. The trip was truly life altering and that is hard to put into words. It was nice to have the group of people we went with to talk about the trip with because no one else really understood what was so great about it other than the weather. A couple of us concluded that Costa Rica wasn't the most beautiful place on the planet, but it was beautiful in its own way with much more of a simple atmosphere than any fancy island resort.

After spending some time reflecting on the trip, I was drawn to why it was the best week of my life and why it was so hard to settle back in. I knew it wasn't just me who would have done almost anything to be back there, but I've always liked to organize my thoughts and understand why I felt a certain way about something. It didn't take me long to realize that it was the first week in almost a year that I was able to forget that I was "Sick". Even though I was still taking my medicine and faithfully applying sunblock to my incision, I essentially forgot because not a single person mentioned my neck and no one asked me what happened to my neck. This was the first time since the operation that I was able to go somewhere and be with complete strangers and not answer the question "what happened to your neck" a single time. For once, I was able to put everything medical aside and just live and that was the most incredible part of the trip. I could lose myself and be a normal teenager free from the struggles, and for the first time in 11 months, be truly happy.

February 27, 2014

Just days after returning from Costa Rica, I found myself back in the airport taking off, only this time, not to Costa Rica. I had made it my goal to miss my flight to Virginia and find my way onto a plane to Central America. Not only did I really not *want* to go to Virginia, having been in the same airports just days ago for the greatest trip of my life made this task even more challenging. I was traveling with my coach as my family could not attend the tournament. I love field hockey, but I still had yet to recover from the trip and I wasn't ready to be leaving my family again. Fortunately, the tournament was only a couple of days and I would be home before I knew it. We got delayed taking off so I decided it would be best to start my homework as I would not be arriving home until late Sunday night and on top of the weekend homework, I was missing 2 days of school. When we finally got on the plane and ready for takeoff, all I could think about was how much I wanted to be at home with my family. Fortunately the flight was short and quick. Once we got in, we checked in to the hotel and tried to find some place to eat. I was traveling with another girl and two coaches. Almost everywhere we went refused to serve people under the age of 21. It was a Thursday night so we were not really sure why that was.

The next morning the tournament started. After the first game, we knew it was going to be a challenge to compete well. The talent was incredible. Day one didn't go too well and day 2 wasn't much better. During one of the games, I was flying out on a corner when I took a drag flick right to the incision. There was no initial pain, rather shock. I jumped in the line of the shot so there was another corner. I flew out again and once again got in the line of the shot. On the third attempt, the ball was finally cleared and I was taken off the court. After a couple of minutes, the shock wore off and the pain set in. I felt like I was back in the hospital the day after surgery hardly capable of movement. I sat out the rest of the game. I don't really know what happened, but I ended up in a total haze with my eyes glossed over and the inability to focus on the next game. At one point in the final game of the day, my coach took me out and pulled me off the bench. She asked me if I was ok and if I still wanted to play. I felt like I was in a daze and I'm surprised I still remember everything. Of course the whole "don't want to make it worse" speech happened. I have just reached the point that I'm sick of sacrificing time and activities and opportunities all around medical decisions.

Once games were over for the night we all headed back to the hotel. I called my mom and told her what happened. There really was nothing to do. It wasn't the first time I have been hit or kicked in the incision. The only thing to do was to ice and take Advil so that's what I did. The tournament was almost over and soon enough I would be home.

The next and final day was a struggle, but when has anything ever been easy? I had already discovered that flying home that night would be miserable. Games finished up and we headed to the airport. I was so close to being home that that fact alone was enough for me to suck it up and make it through. Because of the weather flights were getting all messed up and I just had my fingers crossed we would get out of there and home on time.

After attempting to bang out homework on the flight home in order to make an effort to get some sleep before going back to school, the bumpy flight was over and we finally landed. It was the best feeling seeing my mom and sister at the airport. I knew I was saying goodbye to the airport for quite some time and I couldn't have been happier.

Walking in the doors to my house was oddly liberating. I still wasn't anywhere near ready to go back to school and my life was beyond unorganized.

I already had a countdown going until April break and even then I knew I wouldn't catch a break. Just going to have to go day by day. My schedule was pretty packed and there were some doctors' appointments coming up and my mind was everywhere where it shouldn't have been.

March 4, 2014

After writing dates on my paper all day in school, it hit me what the day meant. Exactly a year ago, the walls around me started caving in. It's bizarre to think of where I was a year ago and where I am now. A year ago, I sat in a doctor's office with no inclination as to where my life would go. I had everything planned out and I had left this out. I remember everything so vividly. Just as I am every day I have a doctor's appointment, I was miserable all day. I could not wait for the appointment to be over and to be walking out of the office for a whole year. I quickly found out that that would not be the case.

One year later, I think of everything that has happened and how it has changed me. I have always believed that an individual is who they are based on the experiences they have encountered. If I could go back a year and change things, would I? I probably would. I know there is no chance that I could prevent what has happened regardless of how hard I tried. With no definitive known cause of Thyroid Cancer, I wouldn't even know where to begin and on top of that, I was perfectly healthy.

After school was over and I had completed most of my homework, I found myself reflecting on the last year and thinking about the road that lay ahead.

March 10, 2014

Heading into the day, I knew it would be a rough and thought filled day. Other than a physical, the appointment itself wouldn't be bad. It was more so the thought of what happened on that day last year. I was by no means looking forward to the appointment or for that matter seeing anyone in the office, but what I was looking forward to was the end when I would have a couple weeks to breathe before my next lab work appointment. Getting through school was a struggle. Time felt like it was moving so slowly and I would never get this appointment over with.

The time finally came. I left school and headed over to the appointment. I really don't understand why I was so nervous for this appointment. It was highly unlikely any bad news would come of this appointment. I walked into the office zoning everything out. They called my name and took me into the room. Of course, it was coincidentally the same room everything began in just a year ago. Before walking in the room, I unconsciously took a moment and stood still in the doorway. The wait felt like hours when in reality it was only 15 minutes. The nurse did her thing and then it was back to waiting for the doctor. Just being in a doctor's office made me sick. This was the first time I would be in the office with most of the staff since the diagnosis. I wanted nothing more than for no one to smother me in their sympathy and everything of that nature.

When my pediatrician walked in, her eyes gave away the type of appointment it would be. I knew I wouldn't make it out of there easily and in a reasonable amount of time. I was no longer an ordinary patient. I like fitting in with the norm and flying under the radar. I care too much about what people think of me to do anything that would draw attention to myself.

And so the appointment began...only not with the usual questions but rather with one of the biggest questions I have grown to hate, "How are you feeling?" Regardless of how I am really feeling, the answer is always "fine," and often I'm told that I am lying. I figure by answering this way, no follow up questions can be asked. She knew I was lying and continued to pry for answers. She knew exactly what to ask to get the answers out of me.

During the appointment, I learned that she still gets my blood work and still communicates with my team at Children's. I knew around the time of surgery she was following me very closely, but I was unaware she was still following me. After surgery, she was in contact with my surgeon who informed her of the pathology reports and how challenging my case was. I really don't care if she knows where I am at, it's fewer questions I have to answer.

After the countless questions that make me beyond uncomfortable, came the best part... the exam. One of the things I hate the most in life is being touched. If it hasn't been terrible in the past years, she made sure it would be worse this year. Being extra careful this year, I quickly became annoyed. Don't get me wrong, I appreciate how careful she was and how she wanted to make sure not to miss anything. If I wasn't already done with doctors before, I definitely was after this. This exam could not have lasted any longer.

Once it was over, she left for a minute and then to conclude the *thrilling* appointment, would be a final question period. I couldn't be more thankful for my pediatrician and what she has done for me. It's blatantly obvious that I am not the easiest person let alone patient to deal with. She followed her gut when she found the initial lump despite thinking it was absolutely nothing. One year later, we can look back on that appointment and remember the words coming out of her mouth and how different the mindset was. Last year, I sat there in disgust that I would have to go for blood work and an ultrasound for what was thought to be "nothing", now a year later, I sit in the exact office thanking my lucky stars and reflecting on everything that came out of "nothing." I can only imagine what would have happened had this not been caught. In a projected year with the disease undiagnosed, the cancer managed to metastasize to more than 25 lymph nodes and cause tumors on my trachea and a solidified thyroid gland. I never got sick and at this point still had no symptoms so I can only conclude that it probably would've been another year before I would have been in the office again. Thinking of what could've been, regardless of the resentment for what has occurred, I truly am thankful for the extra precautions taken that day.

As I have said before, had I been 18, I can't accurately say what I would've decided to do, but I lean towards not accepting the diagnosis and pushing off surgery in a state of denial. I think it's for the best that I was not able to make my own decisions because even a year later, I still haven't accepted the diagnosis and I certainly don't see that happening in the near future. Although my parents ultimately made this decision for me, I don't resent them or their decisions; they were just acting in my best interest and doing what anyone would've done.

Over and over again, my pediatrician has apologized. I understand she is the reason this was caught and the person behind all of this, however, that is no reason to feel guilty and responsible. She didn't do anything wrong, and had I been the ordinary patient, things probably would've been much different. She did and continues to do so much for me. She knew the type of person I would be and immediately gave a list of books to my mom in hopes of keeping me off of the internet. Not only was she right about me and my addiction to the internet and learning more about my diagnosis, she also knew I would read the books that she recommended. What she didn't know is that I went to the internet before I was even diagnosed. I don't like surprises and I was not going to be surprised by anything in the medical field. After this appointment, I am sure she knew that I turned to the internet for answers. She did her job and nothing other than that. She has nothing to be sorry for and I hold no resentment for her. She will always be part of the rough patch, however I appreciate her role during this trying time. but she will be the positive during the trying time.

March 21, 2014

Just as I was starting to move on from Costa Rica and settle back in, the International Club who attended the trip met with our parents to reflect on the trip and show our parents what we did. This was the final hoorah for the trip and I wasn't exactly looking forward to it. With the conclusion of this meeting, Costa Rica would be completely in the past and all it would be is memories. I knew what I felt and I didn't go a day without thinking about it and missing it every second of every day, but I had accepted the fact that it was over and I would make sure I would be back before I saw my last days.

I walked into the meeting and our cult stole all of the desks on the side of the room. We all talked about the trip and what we did while we were there. The chaperones that went on the trip spoke about us and how well behaved we were.

With technological difficulties, we headed down to the computer lab to watch a video with some of everybody's pictures. Our cult sat in the back corner. Sitting with Morgan, Alexa, and Megan looking at these pictures would surely make us emotional. We have been home for exactly a month and things really haven't gotten easier. We still think about it every day and there's not a single day I don't wish I could go back and freeze time. With each picture, we would look at each other with the pained expression. Little did we know that watching the video would not be our only suffering for the night. The chaperones saw the relationship that formed between the group and Jonathan. They had been in contact with him and they worked out a skype reunion. We had no idea and that was the greatest surprise since being in Costa Rica. He single handedly called out our cult and the parents thought it was the funniest thing in the world. We went around the room and each shared our favorite piece of the trip. Everything was so clear and I felt like I was back there and it was the most relaxing feeling.

April 4-5, 2014

If the times weren't busy enough, the college search was on. I headed into the weekend knowing that I would not have any time but I didn't know how bad it would be. One day would be spent at Umass Lowell for a field hockey clinic. I wasn't a fan of the campus before touring, but I really did not like it the second time I went in. The next day would be spent in New York at Siena College. The drive up was much easier than I anticipated. I loved the campus and the field hockey clinic went really well. I knew I could see myself there in a couple years. If I took anything out of this weekend other than the countless hours of field hockey, it would be that I learned just how not ready I am and how much I have to think about.

April 8, 2014

Here's where the days start playing over and over again in my head. Today was my father's birthday. Last year, I wasn't able to celebrate with him. I woke up thinking about the significance of the day and what the upcoming days meant. I remember every little detail about April 8, 2013 and I wish I didn't. I don't have a fear of needles or anything like that, but there's something about the memories of having nine needles longer than your hand stuck into the side of your neck while watching the whole thing happen on the ultrasound screen right next to you that will NEVER leave you. I remember being nervous in school all day before leaving around noon time. Then there was sitting in the waiting room with my mom dreading the procedure. I can look back now and wonder why I was so nervous for something like that because of everything that has happened now. Ask me if I thought I would ever have surgery let alone have surgery for the reasons I did and you'll get the same answer all the time...NEVER. Even with the biopsy and everything, not once did I think of what would transpire. Never once did I imagine myself in this situation. Being so busy kept me distracted from the facts and as much as it stinks not being able to stop for a minute and breathe, this is the best thing for me.

April 9, 2014

Today marks one year since the day my world started falling around me in all directions. This day will always carry its significance. Not only does each year mark progress and new health, but it also marks how much I have grown as a person through this experience. This year, adding to the day was my National Honor Society interview. This could be really good or it could be really bad. I awoke knowing the significance of the day and I was all over the place all day. Nothing seemed to go right from the second I woke up. I was stressed out to the max, per usual, but I just couldn't get myself together long enough before something else would fall apart. That was the theme of the day, and all I could do was be positive and know the day would be over soon enough. For a year now, my motto has always been that I am just another teenager living from day to day. Don't treat me differently and never say anything about me having cancer or my scars or the overused "everything you've been through" crap. I don't want to hear it. I am just like everyone else. I deal with the hell of high school and I participate in sports year round and I am involved with countless school activities and I'm trapped in this never ending cycle of meltdowns and "being done" and all of the other emotions we all face in high school. I can't remember the last time I had a day completely off or a day where I could sit down and not think about the endless list of things I need to get done. But this is not out of the ordinary. Yeah, maybe I am extra hard on myself and I stretch myself too thin or bite off more than I can chew, but that is me, and that's the way I escape from the challenges, even if that means making my life as a busy as an ER physician and being awake and out for 20 out of the 24 hours in a day. These are all choices I make, whether or not they'll make a positive impact on my life, we will see. The day didn't end when the bell went off either. It was a never ending day. After school was track practice, and then STUCO meeting, all topped off by hours and hours of homework and stressing and thus leaving me with no time to myself to think and reflect on everything. If I couldn't escape the aura of the day already, let's add some lab work to the day, why not?

April 10, 2014

I am at the point where all I'm doing is floating through each day with no recollection of things happening. I go from class to class and just sit and stress about everything going on rather than take in the class and focus on what I should be focusing on. April break was just around the corner and my mind was so far out of focus I would tell myself every day that I would organize my life tomorrow, but I would never end up getting to it.

Per usual, the email that would either hold good news or the typical, "let's put more drugs into your system" came in the morning after bloodwork. To no surprise, my numbers were still really off. I expected the usual 25 mcg increase, but this time they decided to increase by 50 mcg. This was the first 50 mcg increase as its typically kept under 25 mcg because you don't want to shock the body by increasing the dose by too much. I was kind of nervous about this and paid extra attention to any side effects that would potentially arise. The only challenge with trying to track symptoms was that I was already overwhelmed and swamped with work that I wasn't sleeping or taking care of my body. I could not differentiate between my condition being caused by side effects or by daily life.

April Break 2014

Finally! A little bit of time to myself, and when I say little, I mean **LITTLE.** Of course, there would be no way there wouldn't be track practice every day...Not that I wanted to not do anything for the week, but I definitely did not want practice plopped in the middle of the day. I planned on organizing my life and doing a lot of cleaning and getting caught up on everything, but per usual, that never happened.

The week flew by and before I knew it, it was time to get ready for school again. I felt like I didn't do anything productive, which I really didn't, but I also knew I didn't sleep an excessive amount or even lay around and waste time. I just have no idea what happened to the 9 days.

During this hiatus, I had the opportunity to attend a New England Revolution game, courtesy of the assistant track coach. I didn't think I would have as much fun as I did. There were four tickets so I had to select wisely. Prior to this, I had started to watch the games and get to see the players. One player who particularly touched my heart was Kevin Alston. Kevin had recently encountered a battle with a rare form of leukemia. With coach Drugan working security that game, we also ended up with field seats rather than club. Being so close to the field was awesome. Not only that, but with the extra minutes added to the clock, a 0-0 draw became a 2-0 Revolution win!! Easily the best day of my vacation!

In preparation to return to school, I sat at my desk with all of my calendars out and while combining them into my master schedule, I realized I would not have a single day off for more than two months. I had not even thought about this prior to recognizing it. I hadn't even acknowledged that not only would I be stuck at the school for practice every day until 5:30-6:00 p.m., but I would also have something after practice almost every day. Realizing this stressed me out beyond reasonable belief. I could not believe my eyes. This stretch of junior year would prove to be the ultimate test.

With the closing of break, summer was one step closer and that was the light at the end of the tunnel.

May 9, 2014

Unlike the rest of the high school girls, I was not looking forward to prom. Everything about the topic just stressed me out and made me angry. Nothing about getting all fancy for 5 hours appealed to me and it was more of a chore than enjoyment. With my luck, I felt that everything that could go wrong, would go wrong.

Getting to the root of my not so optimistic attitude towards the event was a struggle. The only thing blatantly obvious was my lack of comfort. I was not content in my own skin. I'm not okay with how much my body has changed and I'm not comfortable with public view. It all goes back to me caring far too much about what other people think about me.

RANDOM THOUGHTS

My mind plays games with itself. On a good day, I will tell myself that no one knows what has been going on and what they choose to think and talk about is up to them but they have no right to pass judgements. Then on the not so good days, I take that whole mentality and switch it up. People don't know what's going, which believe me, I'm thrilled about, so their lack of knowledge leads them to question and they can see me how they want to see me, but I'll do everything in my power to cover up the scars and hide the pain and discontent. The real question is if and when I'll ever move on and get past this and fully accept that what other people think about me is irrelevant.

- -

Prom overall was a decent experience. It wasn't the best night, but it also wasn't a night I hated. There were laughs, there were smiles, and there was happiness and that's all that matters. After prom was a killer. I was beyond exhausted. I was so used to being able to go nights without sleeping and now being up all hours of the night day in and day out for school and everything else, let alone the fact that my lab work was showing my levels to be increasingly worse, made staying awake a challenge. Attending after prom knowing I would get home with just two hours before I had to be at the school to get on a bus for a track meet was the real killer.

With that being over, I could cross one more thing off of my never ending list!

May 10, 2014

And so the crazy hype surrounding prom just carried on into the next day. I had no desire to get on a bus at 7:30 A.M. and head to Somerville for a track meet. After leaving after prom, I went to Coffee Bean and then went home. It was 5:30 and there was no sense in sleeping for 45 minutes. I fell asleep on the bus and before long I woke up to find that we were lost and had no idea where to go. I obviously was not a happy camper. When we finally got there and got set up, my coach had told me that I had plenty of time to get ready and warm up. He went to get our numbers and was not at the tent when I heard them call the last call for hurdles. I hadn't even been there five minutes yet. The weather was nasty, the timing was nasty, and now I was going to be nasty. Now it may not be his fault that we got lost and got there late, but it is his fault for pushing the bus time back repeatedly. Had we left when we when had originally planned, we would not have had any issues, even if we still got lost. As if I didn't have everything working against me before the race, it started to pour as I was in line to go. Due to our tardy arrival, I did not have the time to put my spikes in my flats. Getting into my blocks, I prepared to slip and not have a good race at one of the toughest meets of the seasons. After I crossed the finish line, I knew that it was the worst race I have ever run in my life so I refused to look at the results. Once the season ended, I looked at the results online and sure enough it was the worst time I have ever gotten in the race. I was already angry but after crossing that finish line I grew more upset. Everything about the poor judgement and unfortunate delay in arrival time made me upset because as a coach you're responsible for the best interest of your athletes and clearly that's not how things went down. The other couple of girls who had qualified for this meet finished their races and then we were ready to head out, only to have to wait an hour for the bus to come. I could not wait to get home and finally sleep after this not so great day.

Mid May

With the change of seasons and being outside for track, I am quickly tanning. One thing has become obvious, as my incision is exposed to the sun, it becomes more visible despite the amount of sunscreen applied. After getting home really late (what's new) one night, my mom made a comment about the increased color of my scar. I had used as many scar removal products and processes they make to try and at least fade it. I had gotten it to a point where the swelling was decreasing and the color was much lighter. Just as I was starting to have it not be the first thing I see when I wake up and last thing I see before I go to bed, it becomes my worst nightmare. After making the comment, I had a nice little heart to heart with my mom about what the action plan would be once I got the all clear. I was happy to hear that she would leave this decision entirely up to me and I would finally have some say in the future. Don't get me wrong, I'm thrilled my parents took control of the situation and didn't let me make all of the decisions for when it comes to anything like this, I encounter issues with tunnel vision and would probably not make the most wise choices.

Each day gets more stressful and I haven't been able to catch my breath and relax for a minute. Between STUCO, track, field hockey, NHS, school, and all of my other activities, I'm out straight for months. It's at the point where my parents are concerned for my health. I've been running myself into the ground since November. The middle of the month was filled with track meets and appointments and meetings and all of those schedule fillers.

As June 27th gets closer, I find myself getting more distracted. On this day, I would find out if all the cancer in my neck was gone and whether I was cancer free or not. I know I have all I can do to get through what I have on my plate right now but I find myself caught up in what may happen. I have been in the best hands I could be in but not having answers has really started to get to me. I've been prepared for this appointment since August so being patient really isn't my thing.

May 15, 2014

I decided to go to tumbling class for the first time in 4 months. Each time I go back, I get increasingly more frustrated. I understand that I have only taken a handful of classes in a year but I can't wrap my head around how much my body has changed and how much I can no longer do. As happy as I am to go in and be able to do something, it sucks something fierce not being able to do everything I could. It's strange to think that I went into retirement almost a year ago and I have only taken about 5 classes since then. I had intentions on going back after the summer, but I was unable to come out of retirement: still thinking about next year and whether or not to come out for my final year.

End of May

The end of May brought the conclusion of the track season that I had been patiently waiting for so long. The end of track season meant one less thing that I had to worry about every day and some more time each day to organize everything and potentially get my homework done sooner and get to sleep. I know I complain about track all of the time, but it's not track that I don't like. I actually really like the sport, but I am never content with my performances. I know I'm not training the way I should be and it's not easy making it through the season with everything working against you: a coach with absolutely no faith in you when you don't have any faith in yourself, a coach who sets me up for failure and does not respect me as a captain, athlete, student, or person for that matter. At this point, there were only a couple of weeks remaining in the school year and the end was in sight: a time I never saw coming.

Medically, May brought a rough patch. My immune system had remained in its weakened state and I went from NEVER getting sick, to getting every virus under the sun. Absolutely exhausted, I continued to carry my schedule while running on empty. My blood levels were getting worse and worse with no explanation why. At this point, we had no answers and the long awaited June appointment was nearing.

First Week of June 2014

The week of firsts were upon us. One year ago this week, the treatment was in the busy stages. Between pre-op, surgery, and the couple of nights spent in the hospital, the week brought a lot of memories up to the surface. After missing the end of sophomore year, believe it or not, it was nice to be able to finish out junior year. In less than two weeks, school would be out and the only thing on my mind would be my upcoming appointment at Children's.

Every day seemed to have some significance. With each day, the school year was keeping me busy and I was finding myself overwhelmed with school and dealing with all of the memories these dates brought. Ironically, *The Fault In Our Stars* movie was being released on June 6th, the date that marked one year of living with a bulging red line across the center of my neck; something that may seem insignificant to some, however being a teenager in high school, the marker brought lot of eyes to my neck and made me uncomfortable more often than not. For 365 days now, I woke up every morning and when I looked in the mirror, this four inch, raised, red line was the first thing I saw. Fortunately, I'm not one of the girly girls who has to wear pounds of makeup and look like I'm heading for the runway every morning because I would have never been able to leave the house.

With my priorities slightly off, I ordered tickets to see the midnight premiere of the movie, despite the fact that it was on a Thursday night, the night before taking two tests and a weekend with SAT's and graduation. After sitting in school all day, I headed to Bentley University for a field hockey game and then when I got home, I had less than half an hour to shower, change, and get out of the house.

The Fault in our Stars held a special spot in my heart. Between reading the brilliantly written story, and having an opportunity to be in the movie, I had been looking forward to this day since the release date was announced. To me, it seemed more than coincidence that the piece would be released on such a significant date.

While my story is nothing like Hazel's, I couldn't help but relate to her story and find myself emotionally connected to her character.

With the approach of June 6th, I found myself thinking a lot and while this movie didn't necessarily take my mind off of cancer, it stole me away from my story and made me hopeful for a better future.

Mid June 2014

My final week of junior year had finally arrived. Junior year was easily the most stressful time of my life. I knew heading into the year that it would be tough, but I never imagined just how tough it would be. Being the person that I am, I took on a tough schedule and filled my plate with three seasons of sports, a club team for field hockey, an executive board seat on the Student Council, and a handful of other extracurriculars. Looking back on my choices, I don't regret them because it kept me occupied and left me little time to think and reflect. Medically, everything was pretty much at a standstill. Aside from appointments here and there and monthly lab work, there were no big dates, only the things that came up with no plans. Without notice, there did end up being a couple of minor medical situations that were taken care of with nothing too invasive. By this point in June, everything was looking up. I had officially made it to senior year and that itself was an accomplishment considering there were points throughout the year I didn't think I would survive the load of cement that junior year dumped on me. As soon as it seemed like I was catching a break with the workload, the load got bigger and bigger. The last couple months I found myself sitting in bed doing homework one minute, and the next I was asleep sitting up. As soon as I caught myself, I would awake to learn that it was the wee hours of the morning and I had fallen asleep while doing homework that was not completed and I would need to be awake in a couple of hours for yet another day at school. Needless to say, each day that passed was a weight off my shoulder and a much needed break was near.

While trying to end the year with solid grades and keep up with the pace of life, I was organizing a Relay for Life team. Carrying a message that meant so much to me, I wanted everything about it to be perfect. The event would take place the day after junior year was completed. Despite the stress of planning this and completing school, I look at the way the dates fell as a gift. Relay For Life surrounds the topic of cancer. Everything you do for this event entails seeing, hearing, or thinking of cancer, which was something I tried to avoid as much as possible. Participating in this event, I knew it would be impossible to avoid the topic, but limiting myself as a target of the event was the goal. I wasn't taking part in this event because I had cancer, but more importantly to help raise funds to support further development in putting an end to a disease that had claimed so many innocent lives.

Being in a location where hundreds of people are spending their time honoring and remembering those who battle and those who have lost their battles to cancer, I imagined I would feel like I was trapped in a hospital with a bunch of sick people. Fortunately, that's not how I ended up feeling.

Once we arrived at the location, we unpacked our cars and set up our site. The event kicked off with a motivational speaker who spoke about her journey with cancer. The speech was followed by the Survivors Lap. I chose not to take part in this for a couple of reasons. I don't think at that point I had accepted that I am a part of that very special population and I refused to label myself. Also, the highly anticipated June 2014 appointment was just under two weeks away and I couldn't risk jinxing myself.

Overall, Relay was a great experience and I got to share it with some of the people who have been there for me during different points. Having seen the bravery of many of the survivors, something inside of me felt different. I was already anxious about my appointment but taking part in the Relay for Life made me so much more optimistic about the outcome of the appointment and I was suddenly overcome with massive amounts of hope.

Once the weekend ended, my focus turned strictly to my appointment. I knew that my battle did not end once I received the highly anticipated good news, but I would be that much closer to putting this all behind and moving on with my life. I wanted so badly for my life to return to the way it was before, but the truth is, this journey has changed me too much to return to who I was before all of this. Every once in a while I find myself desperately wishing none of this ever happened and wondering what would I be like if this didn't happen, but I can't change the past and nothing will ever erase what has occurred since the diagnosis. I had a plan for my life and I knew exactly what would happened when it would happen and where my life would take me. I certainly didn't plan for this. Because of this I learned one of the best lessons that you can't change the past or plan the future, you can only live in the moment and hope for the best.

Junior year was over and I couldn't be more thrilled about that. Sadly, it didn't feel like summer. Our class took a trip down to Newport for senior beach day and then the next day I would leave for the Cape to spend a couple of days with the Student Council executive board at our advisor's house. Despite the warm weather on the beach and good company, I could not enjoy myself because I would have much rather been at home trying to get my life together before the appointment that had me highly distracted.

When I returned home from the Cape, I reunited with my sister that I hadn't seen in week. She was away at Girls State and missed the Relay for Life. This week was the longest we had ever been away from each other and that made it the longest week of my life.

With just a week left before the big day, I got my first day off in months. Finally, a chance to breathe and get some things done for myself. Despite having a couple of days to myself, it wouldn't feel like summer until this appointment was over.

Just days before the big day, I came down with a nasty cough and some breathing difficulties. With a weakened immune system, I had gotten used not only getting sick nearly every time I was around someone sick, but also the frequent trips the PCP's office. Not only did I have yet another respiratory virus, but I was also made aware of some things about Friday's appointment that I really would have been better off not knowing. As it is, it was already evident how much tension and stress I was carrying in my back and neck, but let's just add more stress.

June 26, 2014

What a waste of a day. All 24 hours of June 26th was spent thinking about what the next day would bring. I spent a majority of the time thinking about the logistics of this appointment. I have been waiting for this appointment and the so hoped for good news that it would bring for almost a year now. I could not wait for the day to come, but now that it is here, I don't think I am mentally or emotionally prepared for it. Logistically, I started to question how an ultrasound could lead to the doctors telling me that I am cancer free. How could something that scans pictures of your insides inform me that all of the cancer cells in my body have been terminated, but I'm also not a doctor so I wouldn't have the slightest clue what was coming my way. Despite these questions, I was heading into this appointment with a body consumed by a sense of hope. In the back of my head, I knew that each case is unique, however that didn't stop me from venturing to the world wide web. The fear of the unknown has always been and will continue to be one of my biggest downfalls.

June 27, 2014

The day that I had been waiting for nearly a year had arrived. The wait leading up to this appointment had seemed like years. Whenever someone would ask me how I was doing and what the future plans were, I would respond that I wouldn't know anything until the end of June, which at the time seemed like I was waiting for the impossible to happen. I spent so long waiting for this day to come and now that it had arrived, I wasn't ready to hear the news.

As I laid in bed the night before, my mind was flooded with thoughts. I have dreamed of hearing the words "you're cancer free" as much as anyone dreads hearing the words "you have cancer". I had no idea what this appointment would be like other than the fact that I would have an ultrasound. Per usual, my curiosity and lack of understanding sent me to the internet, which I learned the hard way is a fear trap. Each person's case is unique and no results are typical so the resorting to the internet is a nasty habit.

I woke up in the morning feeling like a black cloud was hanging over my head and filled with nerves. The fear of the unknown has always been one of my biggest downfalls. I completed my usual Boston day routine; I got up, got ready, and got in the car.

The drive into Boston that day felt like an eternity. I went to bed with anxiety and woke up with it and I knew that it would not cease until I got the news I had been waiting for almost a year. The turn on to Longwood Ave marked what I hoped to be the final leg of the journey towards health.

I walked into the office at 333 Longwood Ave. to meet with the nurse before heading over to Brigham and Women's for the ultrasound. I filled out the paperwork and played the waiting game I have become so good at. Once I got into the room, the nurse put a cream and some tape on my incisions and sent me across the way to the Brigham. For anyone that knows me, they understand I cannot stand my neck being touched or having any type of fabric or material touching it. While walking over to the next appointment, this cream and tape on my neck had me unjustifiably angry. I felt like gagging every other second and I could not distract myself for long enough to allow this sensation to vacate. Yet again, the wait was longer than anything I have ever experienced. I had forgotten what I was really doing in that waiting room and the only thing I could focus on was the second they would pull this stuff off of my neck. Finally my name was called and I could relax, only until I realized that I wasn't waiting just to take this off of my neck, but rather to determine where I stood on my journey through cancer.

I hoped to have the same technician as the first time, but I didn't, however she was equally good. The cold and sticky gel was placed on my neck and it was time. I tried not to watch the screen but temptation sunk in and I could not help myself. In contrast to last time, I could not figure out whether the news would be good or the unthinkable. The technician left and said Dr. Smith would be in. The technician, the head of radiology and Dr. Smith all came back in and I slipped into negativity, at that point the news couldn't be good. The head of radiology took another look and that's when I was positive it could not be good. Dr.Smith had that look in her eye and my suspicions were confirmed, all that was left to do was say the words. Dr. Smith had her hand on my shoulder and glanced down at me from time to time spending the rest of her time in the room looking over at the screen. The three of them left to take another look at the scans.

Upon their entrance back to the room, she began to tell me that I had more lymph nodes that appeared cancerous and then my mom entered from the other door. I knew that there was one lymph node because I had found it back in August and the surgeon had said that it was not cancerous when they closed during surgery. And just days ago, another doctor told me it didn't have any ugly features. Therefore, I got my hopes up sky high that this would be my day. The day I finally got good news. The day I could breathe and start to get back to the person I was before all of this happened. I have never been the most outspoken or set my hopes up, but for the first time, I felt victim to high hopes.

Dr. Smith wanted to biopsy one of the lymph nodes she found on the ultrasound, and should the results show malignancy, I would be back very soon for another surgery. I had never felt so defeated before in my life.

While my mom signed the consent form, Dr. Smith set up for the biopsy and I stared off into space angrier than ever. Morgan decided she could not watch this so she left the room and headed back to the waiting room. I just wanted to feel myself again and have the energy to do everything I did just over a year ago. It had been 14 months since the last biopsy, but I had a good idea what to expect. The lymph node she chose to biopsy was a rolling node and that made it tough. The team assembled, I rolled over to my side, and the ultrasound was placed on the lymph node just before she placed in the numbing medicine. After a handful of needles into and out of, the pressure and pain was almost unbearable. With only two samples left, my legs were shaking and the tears began to roll down my face. Once the bandage was placed, I could sit up and make an attempt at relaxing. The samples were labeled and shipped off to pathology and chemistry for a thyroglobulin reading. There were no results, but she was adamant that I would be back for surgery very shortly. Even if this node came back benign, there was an ever larger and uglier one resting on my jugular that would need to be biopsied so even if the miracle happened and this one was not cancerous, the journey wasn't over. There were more lymph nodes on the other side of my neck that she would need to prove to the surgeon should be removed, so that may mean more than one more biopsy.

Despite the possibilities of there being more cancer living in my body, my hopes were still high and I couldn't wait to be cleared, have a good summer, and enjoy my senior year! It was almost one o'clock in the afternoon, I hadn't eaten anything all day and I had to go for lab work. My head was full of pressure from the biopsy and after the lab work, I was dizzy and out of it. Walking out of the hospital was both the best and worst feeling. The ride home was long and when I got home, I took a nap in the screenhouse, woke up for a couple of hours, and headed to bed for the night. This appointment symbolized where my real journey would begin, and just how hard I would have to fight to find my way back to serenity.

ADVICE (14 MONTHS POST DIAGNOSIS)

I will probably spend the rest of my life learning more about myself and taking more lessons from my journey through cancer, but for now, I leave you will the most important of the lessons I learned through the first 14 months of my journey.

My number one piece of advice for someone of any age, any background, or any diagnosis is to **allow yourself to feel**. Trying to organize every single thing you feel into little boxes will only create more unnecessary stress. Let yourself have emotions and find the people in your life that you can share these with. One of my biggest regrets is pretending I didn't have any emotions. I trudged through everyday pretending like I didn't have cancer and convincing myself that I was the typical teenager in high school.

Write! If you struggle with talking to someone, keep a journal, blog, or just write yourself emails. I have no idea where I would be if I did not turn to writing after my diagnosis. It is ok to put your story out there. You had a standoff with cancer, you are a superhero in so many ways.

DO NOT believe everything you read on the internet! The internet is a dangerous place for medical research. There are so many scholastic sites out there that are written by medical professionals that can offer you legitimate information. No two cases of any disease are the same and therefore you can't predict how you will square off with cancer. Reading the information or watching videos put out there by people lacking certification will only freak you out. In the days leading up to any type of treatment or procedure, I found myself turning to the internet more frequently. Do not do this. I put myself in a rough place and almost everything I read or watched is not what actually occurred.

Surround yourself with people who are only going to build you up. Wasting your time on people who spend their time tearing you down is silly. What you need in the face of adversity is support and these people are doing the exact opposite of that. In trying times, I promise you that you will discover the people that will support you unconditionally and be there for you no matter what time of the night it is.

Love your scar(s). It's a piece of you that will always be a constant reminder of your strength and bravery. No one can tell you that you do not possess strength and bravery. Your scar may be the first thing that you see when you look in the mirror and the last thing you feel before falling asleep. As much as you may say you want to forget your journey through cancer, there will inevitably be a piece of you that holds on to whatever emotions this journey may have brought you. Don't change your scar to make anyone else happy. I have scars and marks everywhere that remind me of who I am today and all that I have been through. In the beginning, I was willing to do anything to get rid of my scars, but now, I believe that they are part of me for a reason and I will wear them proudly.

Know that it is ok to cry. You are only human. Don't try and be a hero. Repressing all of your emotions, while at the time may seem the better choice, in the long run, will only prove to be a mistake. It took me days before I cried following my diagnosis. Being 16 and healthy, my only thought was how could this be happening. You don't have to be strong 24 hours a day, seven days a week.

Be bold. Go out during the week, hang out with friends and family, etc.; If you don't get something done, the world is not going to end. Overloading yourself with work isn't going to get rid of your cancer. Do things that make you happy and things that create memories that will last a lifetime. Keeping yourself up all night to finish work or sitting there stressing about the endless list of things you have to get done by a deadline is pointless. Remove all unnecessary stress from your life! I guarantee you it will instantly make you feel better.

Don't settle with doctors you do not feel comfortable with. You need to have complete faith in your doctor so if there is even the smallest piece of you that does not feel comfortable, go somewhere else. There are so many doctors out there that there is absolutely one that is right for you.

Ask questions. Most often, the patient does not have a medical degree. Even if you feel like an idiot, ask questions and understand what is going on. Having an understanding of what is going on will eliminate the fear of the unknown and alleviate some anxiety.

Being 14 months outside of my diagnosis, the final piece of advice I can give you is to **stop worrying about what everyone else thinks or says and instead do the things that make you happy.** Having faced cancer, you are of a special breed. Go after the things you have always wanted to but have never had the confidence to. You waste time worrying about what others say and think about you. Spend that time making yourself happy. As a wise woman once told me, "You only live in this moment once. Don't waste your time doing things that you really don't need to but feel obligated to do. Spend that time hanging out with friends on a school night, watching trashy lifetime movies and eating ice cream, and just doing the things that make you smile. You're not going to remember doing a homework assignment or studying for a test, you're going to remember the things that brought joy to your life."

Email: livingwiththeribbon2015@gmail.com

ABOUT THE AUTHOR

MacKenzie Greenberg is a recent graduate of Hopedale Junior-Senior High School who lives in Mendon, Massachusetts with her parents, Kim and Alan, twin sister, Morgan, and older sister, Lindsey. Growing up she was a dedicated gymnast and dancer with aspirations to perform in Cirque du Soleil until diagnosed with cancer at the age of 16. A three season athlete, MacKenzie acquired 10 high school varsity letters in field hockey, track and field, and was recognized as a League All-Star in both track and field hockey during her 4 years at Hopedale Junior-Senior High School. Recruited for field hockey, MacKenzie will be a member of the entering freshman Class of 2019 at the Stonehill College where she plans to pursue a major in biology, and a minor in psychology with a graduate plan to become a Physician's Assistant. With a strong desire to enter the field of Pediatric Oncology, MacKenzie hopes to use her life experiences as a patient at Boston Children's Hospital and Brigham and Women's to help other people through their battle with cancer.

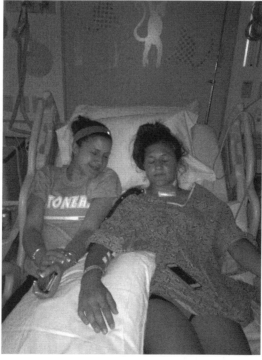

21417565R00077

Made in the USA
Middletown, DE
29 June 2015